69 Ways
To Better Relationships, Sex and Love

69 Ways To Better Relationships, Sex and Love

With 43 poems, photographs and a few laughs...

by R. Ray Barnes

Roberto Casanova & Julie Lovelace
Photography by LaSalle Barnes

In Spirit INTERNATIONAL, LLC

Copyright © 2009, 2013 by R. Ray Barnes

All rights reserved. No part of this book may be reproduced or transmitted in any form or by any means, electronic or mechanical, including photocopying, recording, or by any information storage and retrieval system without permission in writing from the publisher.

Notice

This publication is intended as a reference book only, not as a medical manual. It contains the opinions and ideas of its author and is meant to provide helpful and informative material on the subject matter covered. It is sold with the understanding that the author and publisher are not engaged in rendering professional services via the book. It is not offered as a substitute for any treatment that may have been prescribed by your doctor. If you suspect you have a medical problem that requires personal assistance or advice, a competent professional should be consulted. Statements regarding any guarantees, implied or otherwise are made solely for literary and dramatic purposes. The author and publisher make no guarantees and specifically disclaim any responsibility for any liability, loss or risk, personal or otherwise, occurred as a consequence, directly or indirectly, of the use and application of any of the contents of this book. Please be advised that this book contains material of a sexual nature and may not be suitable for children. We encourage all to use condoms and practice safe sex.

First Printing, 2013

Mail requests for permission to make copies of any part of this work to:
In Spirit INTERNATIONAL, LLC
P. O. Box 571633 • Los Angeles, CA 91357

Or Email us: Love@69WaysTheBook.com

Library of Congress Control Number: 2009910874

ISBN 13: 987-0-9842535-1-7

Printed in the United States of America

Poetry: *Bianca Baker, R. Ray Barnes, Roberto Casanova, Denise L. Cook, Julie Lovelace, Leslie E. Pogue, Saphron, Lisa Stout and Toi.*
Healthful Hints: *R. Ray Barnes,* Commentary: *Karen M. Webster, M.D.*
Photography: *LaSalle Barnes,* © 2009 by R. Ray Barnes and LaSalle Barnes
Models: *Style Bell, Jasmine Smith, Bryan Au, Keiko Kawamura, Damon Ritchie, Nathalie Ritchie, Nazanin Mandi, Porfirio Hernandez, Manny Cazz, Robert & Yvonne Barnes, Kourtney Delette and Sia Semos.*
Cover Design & Graphics: *R. Ray Barnes, LaSalle Barnes and Ghislain Viau*
Interior Design and Layout: *Ghislain Viau*
Editor: *Ron Kenner,* Associate Editor: *Lois E. Moore and Cecelia E. Finney*

*Dedicated in memory of
Lois E. Moore.*

*To my mother (Yvonne Barnes), and my father (Robert Barnes),
married for over 60 years, who taught me my first and lasting lessons
regarding love. There is no better teacher than a good example.*

*To the extraordinary women that I have been so blessed
to love and have been so honored to be loved by....
I want to thank you for allowing me to share my love with you.*

*To **Receive** love
is the most wonderful and gratifying of all life's experiences,
surpassed only by the feeling you get
when you **Give** love...*

—*R. Ray Barnes*

"Live, laugh and love together…"

"Laughter is the fuel that warms the heart
and keeps the love flame burning…"

Contents

Note: The numbers on the left begin the count from 1 to 69. All poems in the book are highlighted in gray. Letters, A. B. C ... identify the "Healthful Hints" and a complete list can be found on page xx. An entire alphabetical listing of the poems can be found at the end of this Contents.

Foreword *by Toi*	xiii
Preface *by R. Ray Barnes*	xvii
Healthful Hints	xix
Introduction Take I: Making Love: Physical or Mental?	1
Introduction Take II: Having Sex: Men vs. Women	9
Introduction Take III: The Rate-A-Date Scale (RAD)	23
The RAD Scale Questions Chart	25
The RAD Scale Hearts Chart	27
How Your Date Rates On The RAD Scale	27
The RAD Comparison Chart	28

Chapter One: Love Rules of the Road

1.	Check The *"Whether"* Conditions	31
2.	Don't Forget Your Safety Kit	32
3.	Have A Trip Plan	34
4.	Fasten Your Seat Belts	34
5.	Adjust Your Mirrors	34
6.	Obey the Speed Limit	35

7.	Learn to Yield	35
8.	Watch for Turn Signals, U-Turns and Backup Lights	36
9.	It's Slippery When Wet	37
10.	Obey the Traffic Signal Lights	38

Chapter Two: Licking the Myths

11.	Size Does Matter... Right?	41
12.	Big Hands, Big Feet, Big D...?	44
13.	Breast Size, The Bigger the Better?	45
14.	Don't Let Her Body Size Fool You	47
15.	No Sex Period!	50
16.	Age Ain't Nothin' But a Number	51
17.	Douche, Douche In the Bush?	54
18.	PMS: Is It Is or Is It Ain't?	54
19.	Masturbation Will Make You Go Blind	55
20.	Hell Hath No Fury Like A Woman Scorned?	58

Chapter Three: Things To Say or Do Before Sex

21.	Know Thy Self and Love Thy Self	66
22.	In Love We Trust	67
23.	Looks Can Be Deceiving	70
24.	Foreplay Is All Day, 24/7	73
25.	Guys, Ladies Love to Receive Flowers	74
26.	Ladies, Your Hands and Feet Can Be Such a Sexy Turn-on	76
27.	Guys Compliment the Ladies	76
28.	Learn To Be A Good Kisser	77
29.	Guys, She Doesn't Owe You Anything	79
30.	Honesty Is the Best Policy, So Ladies Don't Lead Him On	79
31.	Lights, Camera, Action!	80
32.	Ladies, Don't Say, "I'm Going To Give You Some"	80

33. Guys, Always Dress Nice, Smell Good and Be Neat ... 81
34. Guys and Ladies, Learn To Dress Appropriately ... 82
35. Save A Tree, But Whack Your Bush ... 83
36. Ladies, If You're Gonna Dress the Part, Then Play the Part ... 83
37. Learn How To Give and Receive Compliments ... 84
38. Exercise Your Way To Better Orgasms ... 85
39. Don't Stop Playing With Toys ... 87
40. Should You Have Sex On the First Date? ... 89

Chapter Four: Things To Say or Do During Sex

41. Always Be Willing To Give More Than You Receive ... 93
42. Guys, Sex Is Really All About Pleasing Her ... 94
43. Never Keep A Lady Waiting ... 95
44. Always Be Clean, Smell Good and Have Fresh Breath ... 96
45. Your Mind Is On Vacation ... 98
46. Sometimes You Have Sex, F#@k, Make Love ... 99
47. Guys, Don't Be In Such A Hurry ... 100
48. Guys, As A Rule, Be Gentle ... 100
49. If It Don't Fit Don't Force It ... 102
50. During Lovemaking Learn To Listen ... 103
51. Shut Up Already and Listen! ... 103
  ABC's To Better Communication ... 106
52. Be Spontaneous and Creative ... 112
53. Tell Your Lover You Care About Him or Her ... 118
54. Guys, If You Have A Bout of Premature Ejaculation ... 119
55. Ladies, Don't Complain If Your Lover Can't Get It Up ... 119
56. A Winner Never Quits and A Quitter Never Wins ... 120
57. Give Him A Quickie, and Guys Go As Long As She Wants You To ... 121
58. Occasionally, Give Without Being Asked ... 122

59.	Learn How To Give and Receive Oral Sex	123
60.	You Can't Lose With the Stuff I Use	127
61.	One Good Turn Deserves Another	128
62.	Don't Be Afraid To Lose Control and Let Go	128

Chapter Five: Things To Say or Do After Sex

63.	Keep It Real	133
64.	Men, If You Snooze You Lose	134
65.	Guys Shut Up! Ladies Speak Up!	136
66.	Don't Expect Your Lover To Love You the Way You Would	138
67.	Measuring A Man's Love Is Different Than A Woman's Love	139
68.	Being Turned On and Turned Off Sexually	141
69.	What's Love Got To Do With It?	146

Afterword	151
Afterthought	159
About The Authors	175
About The Contributors	177
About The Poets	178
Acknowledgments	181
Sources, Suggested Reading and Related Web Sites	183
Song of Solomon	187
Recognizing True Love	190
Final Thought: How Do You Know You're In Love?	191
Contact Us	193

List of Poems
Alphabetical Order

Title	Author	Page
After You Cum…	J. Lovelace	31
As We	D. Cook	129
Blanket Of Love	B. Baker/R.R. Barnes	76
Blinking Constantly…	R.R. Barnes	36
Can't Find The Words	R. Casanova	116
Definition Of Love	R.R. Barnes	162
Do I Ever Cross Your Mind?	R.R. Barnes	140
Entwined In love	R.R. Barnes	137
Extra Sensory Perception	R.R. Barnes	6
Finding Love	R.R. Barnes	182
Free Falling…	J. Lovelace	154
Haunted Dreams	J. Lovelace	61
Her Kiss	R.R. Barnes	78
I'm…Yours	B. Baker/R.R. Barnes	74
If Life Is About What Is?	R.R. Barnes	41
If You "Cum" In Love…	R.R. Barnes	133
Infinite Voyage	R.R. Barnes	39
It Doesn't Matter	D. Cook	86
Learning	R.R. Barnes	xviii
Let Me Say… I Love You	Toi	158
Looks Can Be Deceiving	R.R. Barnes	72
Love	R.R. Barnes	151
Love's Harvest	J. Lovelace	128
Love Is Never Having To Say…	R.R. Barnes	148
Making Love Mentally	L. Stout	3
Men vs Women	R.R. Barnes	9
Message Of Love, The	R.R. Barnes	1
New Diet	J. Lovelace	126
Now Hear This	J. Lovelace	104

Nutcracker Sweet	J. Lovelace	120
Rainy Afternoon	B. Baker/R.R. Barnes	102
Relayshunship	R. Casanova	82
Silent Conversations	R.R. Barnes	112
Silent Night	R. Casanova	114
Stop, Look and Listen	R.R. Barnes	135
The Hunted	L. E. Pogue	11
Thoughts Of You	R.R. Barnes	156
Trying To Cure My Weakness	R. Casanova	80
Wake Up Call	Saphron	127
Wherever Your Love Takes Me	R.R. Barnes	173
While You Are There	J. Lovelace	65
Yes! Right There	D. Cook	122
Your Love	R.R. Barnes	93

The Hunted © 2005 By Leslie E. Pogue.
Wake-Up Call © 2002 By Saphron,
Conch Shell Press P.O. Box 95276, Seattle, WA 98145-2276
Let Me Say I Love You © 2009 By Toi
It Doesn't Matter, Yes! Right There and As We © 2003 By Denise L. Cook,
www.theoraclespeaks.info
Reprinted by permission

Foreword

If it's true that the four elements, water, fire, air and earth are the driving forces of nature, then it's certainly true that human sexuality is the driving force of humankind. Far beyond the purpose of procreation, the pursuit of the all-powerful orgasm, or even denial of it, consumes every aspect of every human culture. We define morality or lack of it by the how, when, and with whom it's pursued. More often than not, the way we style our hair, decide what to wear, or what car we drive can be traced to how we present ourselves for the sole purpose of who we attract and ultimately with whom we share the sexual experience.

In western society it has always been fascinating to me how, more openly than almost any other culture, we brandish our sexuality as commercially as we do a brand of soda pop; and yet we pretend it's the least important matter on our agendas. Almost with shame we pretend that the primary pursuit is non-existent, although evidence to the contrary is all around us. Not many realize and few people are honest about the amount of time, energy and effort that they invest in their sexual selves; we even scorn those who openly admit it's their favorite pastime.

We affix labels and pass judgment on others according to how we perceive their sexual interest, preferences and appetites. We feel guilty about our own pursuits if we sense they won't withstand the scrutiny of others. We even deceive ourselves about what we do, have done, or would be willing to do; yet no fear of judgment by man or God seems to deter, in any culture, the stark reality of our human need for sexual expression. Amazingly we will research and study almost any given subject of interest or concern, yet—unless, of course, we consider *Playboy, Penthouse* or *Hustler* Magazine read at least once by most men, (with the 'reading part' in question)—few have ventured to actually read information on human sexuality. Seemingly off the beaten path, though not really, I was amazed to discover the number of cookbooks and recipe cards that my grandmother owned. I'd always thought of her as a very natural amazing cook who needed nothing more than desire and ingredients to whip up a fabulous meal at a moment's notice. Apparently she understood what anyone who is really good at anything knows—with exposure to the ideas of others, you can always be better at what you do. This evidently applies to many areas outside of the kitchen.

We don't start out taking "Sex 101" classes—most of us dove into our first sexual encounters with little more than schoolyard talk or romance novels as our only knowledge of what to do, expect, or feel. We can spend years without figuring out what works for our partners or us. Some people actually find themselves married with children, divorced, and still have no solid handle on their sexual selves. Some of us may have identified who we are in our *own* sexual context, yet remain clueless about the opposite sex. Others of us may have figured out the magical dance with one person, but can't manage to find our rhythm with another.

Sex, the alpha of life, like life, is and should be *ever evolving*. We are not the same sexual beings in our 20s as we might find ourselves in our 30s or 40s. Fluid like water, the shape of our sexual selves alters with a range as vast as our minds and as deep as our emotions. What you enjoy today may not be the same turn-on five years from now. Things you perhaps ruled out and would never have considered ten years ago could become very appealing and yield pleasures untold for you at this moment in time. The key would be in remaining open-minded and ever in touch with your sexual personality—to accept, respect and nurture it as you would any other aspect of your being.

That's the beauty of *69 Ways To Better Relationships, Sex and Love*; whether you fancy yourself as the possessor of "whip-appeal," if you've decided to take your sexual expression to a higher level, or if you still haven't figured out what all the fuss is about, there's something for you within these pages.

Poignant, and at times hilarious and shooting straight from the hip, (no pun intended) author, poet, record producer and screenwriter R. Ray Barnes along with his alter egos Roberto Casanova and female-side kick Julie Lovelace brings delightful enlightenment to every aspect of the sexual experience, including putting several rumors and myths to bed!

69 Ways To Better Relationships, Sex and Love can be used as a "how to" or as a "refresher guide." It can be shared reading with a partner and the catalyst for some wonderful dialogue or intimate activity. So, as serious as you may be or as playful as you need to be, you'll surely walk away with a chuckle in your heart, a smile on your face, and a sense of comfort in knowing you're a more *aware* lover.

Toi

R. Ray Barnes, Author

Preface

Sex vs. Love

You may be surprised to find that 69 Ways To Better Relationships, Sex and Love is a lot more *mentally* gratifying and insightful than one might expect. It very simply, in a fun-to-read and sometimes lighthearted way, shares with you vital information that helps you understand love and sexual relationships and how to make them better!

Though sex and love are often tossed into the same salad, they don't always go well together. One should understand that sex is quite different from love, just as women are quite different from men. While sex seems to be paramount on a man's mind, women think about sex a lot less. Some surveys indicate that men think about sex every five seconds, while women average only several times a day—which begs the question, "What's love got to do with it?" We must realize that the mere physical act of sexual intercourse, "having sex" or what some call "making love," no matter how emotional, sincere or well intended, at best can only serve, though not always, as one of the many *expressions* of love, such as treating one with kindness and caring for or about someone. Sex in any form is *not* love. Nor does a couple's desire to have sex, saying, "I love you," and/or marrying someone prove love's existence. Don't be disillusioned! Love is a matter beyond the physical and beyond the mind; it emanates from deep within the *heart, spirit* and *soul*... and is only *expressed* by the body. Unless it manifests spiritually from the inside out, it is not true love; when you come to recognize, understand and *feel* true love, you will be blessed to know what it's like to experience heaven on earth.

There Is More To Love Than Sex

Sex is no doubt wonderful! But endeavor to keep sex in its proper perspective. As you enjoy *69 Ways To Better Relationships, Sex and Love*, keep in mind that there is more to love than sex. Many couples are no longer able to engage in sex (for medical reasons, age, etc.) yet they remain very much *in* love and still *make* love to each other—that's because, contrary to the belief of many, you **can** *make* love without having sex—an idea supported by a survey published in the January/February 2010 issue of *AARP The Magazine*, which found that 77% of American respondents said, "True love could exist without a radiant sex life." However, *69 Ways To Better Relationships, Sex and Love*, will show you how to build a better, more meaningful relationship so that you may experience great sex even if you're not *in* love and experience great love even if you're not having sex. Though ultimately, it may well lead you to the greater experience—that of enjoying great sex and great love simultaneously.

R. Ray Barnes

Learning

Lessons
are about the past...
Acting
is about the now...
Planning
is about the future...
but,
Learning
is all the time!

R. Ray Barnes

Healthful Hints

We found it impossible to have a book about sex and better lovemaking without highlighting the role that good health plays. Good health makes for good sex, and good sex makes for good health. Because good health is *so* important in helping couples achieve great sex on a more consistent basis, *69 Ways To Better Relationships, Sex and Love* features a series of easy to find *Healthful Hints*, with special commentary by our Physician Consultant, Karen M. Webster, M.D., MPH, that will supply you with tips on how to stay in good health and keep your sexual experiences pleasurable and enjoyable.

In a March 2005 article, *Why Sex Is Good for Your Health*, eDiets staff writer, Glenn Mueller stated, "There is an increasing amount of research to support the idea that sex is good for your health. Some public health experts even say that sex is as important to your health as diet and exercise." In that same article, Mueller quotes best-selling author and nationally syndicated radio personality, Dr. Dean Edell, who adds, "A healthy sex life may not only be a sign of good health, but also a cause of it."

According to bodyandfitness.com, "Sex stimulates the release of various chemicals such as endorphins. These endorphins encourage deeper sleep, relaxation and a better sense of being." The site further notes, "Sex improves blood flow to the skin and helps keep it more vibrant, supple and healthy. That goes for other parts of the body as well." Yet, if you're feeling bad, it's hard to have good sex.

It seems safe to say we all realize that exercise, good nutrition, and maintaining good health overall is *good* for us, and, as the milk commercial slogan says, it "does a body good." And, although in our younger years we may not have readily noticed the benefits of exercise and good nutrition, or the lack thereof as we get older, Dr. Webster emphasizes that we must pay closer attention. Good health not only affects us physically, but emotionally, mentally and sexually as well.

When you're in good health, you feel better about yourself no matter your age. Nothing beats confidence; it gives you that inner and outer glow that makes people notice you. And with the added energy you get from feeling good, we like to say, "The better you feel, the better you thrill." A satisfying sex life has much less to do with your age than with your state of health and state of mind.

So as you're enjoying *69 Ways To Better Relationships, Sex and Love*, please pay attention to these Healthful Hints and use them to help you maintain a healthier and sexier lifestyle.

No.	Healthful Hints Topics	Page
A.	Sexually Transmitted Diseases (STDs)	32
B.	Vaginal Dryness	37
C.	Prostate Health	42
D.	Breast Examinations	45
E.	Obesity and Weight	48
F.	Vaginal Bleeding	50
G.	Colon Health	52
H.	Heart Disease and Stroke	88
I.	Smoking and Sex	97
J.	High Blood Pressure	101
K.	Premature Ejaculation	115
L.	Erectile Dysfunction	117

Introduction Take I

Making Love: Physical or Mental?

Making love should be one of the most enjoyable, most beautiful and most gratifying interactions we share with each other. It has the ability to stimulate and electrify every nerve ending in our bodies and give us sensory pleasures beyond our wildest imaginations. It can heal, thrill and reveal joy we never knew we had. For the most part, we can experience this ecstasy by simply practicing good communication, being cooperative, freeing our minds and allowing ourselves to be intimate and by exercising an unselfish desire to please our lovers. However, because it sounds so simple, many take it for granted; unaware that pleasing one's lover is so much more than merely engaging in the physical act of sexual intercourse. Sex is a mental act as well.

The Message Of Love

The **Message** of **Love** comes not from the multitude of **Words** that are **Spoken**, but is hidden in the **Silence** which lies in between the **Words**.

R. Ray Barnes

According to Yogi Bhajan, in the *Kundalini Research Institute International Teacher Training Manual Level 1* for professional Yoga instructors, "The mind is the biggest sexual organ. It stimulates the body by using fantasy, projection, and remembrance." Also, in *Tantric Secrets, 7 Steps To The Best Sex Of Your Life*, author Cassandra Lorius states, "Your mind is the key to the best sex in your life. You have the capacity to give yourself an orgasm through the power of your mind. Some people can have an orgasm while being pleasured; some from just thinking about their pleasure."

So, as soon as we understand that making love does not begin with the physical act of sexual intercourse and does not end when the physical act is over, we'll be on our way to experiencing what *true* "lovemaking" is really all about. When putting your mind to use while having sex, you can learn to become sexually satisfied as opposed to being merely satisfied with having sex.

Many don't realize that we spend very little time in bed actually making love. Most of our time is spent mentally preparing for it and trying to figure out what to do afterward, so that we may get to do it all over again.

As the doctrine of karma emphasizes and as Isaac Newton has said, "For every action, there is an equal and opposite reaction." Therefore, our reactions to, and our attitudes and feelings toward the actions of our lovers, can and do make their way into our bedrooms affecting what we will and will not do sexually. Certain types of behaviors demonstrated by our lovers throughout the day may affect whether in the evening we will be comfortable and relaxed, open and honest, loving and caring…. The human psyche and emotions are very complicated. Many things that affect us sexually may seem totally unrelated on the surface.

We must understand that we make love to *people*, and their *actions* define who they are as people. Therefore, we indirectly make love to their actions. This not only includes things we say and do to our lovers personally and directly, but includes things we say and do to others that our lovers observe. Thus, we must be mindful of all of our actions, because they may well, in one way or another, affect our sex lives. Here again, Yogi Bhajan teaches, "Sex is everything. Sex is nothing." In the *Kundalini Research Institute International Teacher Training Manual Level 1*, he asserts, "When a couple wants to have a good sexual relationship, a good day-to-day relationship with effective clear communication is essential. The heart-to-heart basics cannot be missing. Sex cannot solve problems or create trust or replace open communication. Sex does not just happen in bed. It starts in the day-to-day life: how we are, how we speak, how we hear, and how we live for each other. Sex is the greatest treat we can share."

So it's just as much and sometimes even *more* important—what we think and do before and after sex—as is what we do during intercourse. What we think and do before and after sex can have a profound effect on the sexual act itself. Actually, what we do before, during and after is really all part of *one* three-act performance. Having an understanding of that principle is the first step on our journey to becoming better lovers and ultimately leads to better lovemaking. But remember, when boarding a love flight—leave your 'baggage' behind.

Making Love Mentally

My Flesh—screams
My Muscles—ache
My Sexuality—lays back
As I wrestle with My Lust...
You have only looked at Me and yet we have made love...
I've been touched by
Your Eyes, Your Heart, Your Soul...
My Spirit—intercoursed
Briefly with Your Life...
Just enough for You to escape with Me Into Us

Lisa Stout

Warning! Warning! Warning!

We want to make you aware right from the start that this book may not be suitable reading for everyone. We want to warn those of you, who are faint of heart, that the "F" word is used a couple of times to more accurately describe a feeling, an emotion and a sexual act in a way that no other word can. We hope to offend no one; however, if we do, please understand we are discussing intimate sexual acts involving adults and not Sylvester and Tweety Bird.

Further, we do require a few things of you and highly recommend these before you attempt to read this book. First, you must remove your underwear from your butt-crack so you can relax. Second, though the information is serious, our approach is lighthearted and fun and at times hilarious. So it's okay if you laugh out loud. In an effort to get our point across, we sometimes quote master teachers, intellectuals and philosophers like Kahlil Gibran, author of *The Prophet*, Yogi Bhajan, Founder of the *Kundalini* (Yoga) *Research Institute*, international author and motivational speaker, Dr. Deepak Chopra, the *Holy Bible* and others.

We've also referenced many sex experts in the field, made use of the Internet, various sex manuals and research data from major studies; and when necessary, we even use street vernacular. We're not trying to win a *Pulitzer Prize*. Our goal is to achieve a *real* sense of understanding and comprehension.

Although some basic education would be helpful, a Ph.D., Master's Degree, or Bachelor's Degree is not required. However, we do strongly recommend and suggest that you possess at least one of the following: a penis, a vagina, a tongue, a mouth, a breast or two, an ass, or a desire to see one, touch one, feel one, hold one, kiss one, lick one, suck one, bite one, massage one or just wish to be one. If you meet any of those requirements we encourage you to continue. If you *do not* meet any of the requirements listed above, then you should immediately throw this book to the floor and call *911*, because you have a much more serious problem than we care to address here!

This book is *not* meant to be a reference manual that you put on the shelf and refer to only when you're having problems. It's not filled with useless medical jargon and cosmic bio-rhythmic charts explaining when it's the best time for you to have sex. Nor does it answer questions like: What is the missionary position and does it have anything to do with church? Why does my penis shrink in water? Is my vagina related to my angina? Does oral sex have anything to do with Oral Roberts? And so on... No! This book is meant to serve as a *quick* and *easy* practical guide to help you better understand love, improve your intimate relationships and achieve greater sexual pleasure and satisfaction right now—and on a continuous basis, regardless of where you are in your present relationship. Everyone will be able to benefit from the information contained herein—whether you are just discovering sex for the first time, or are a Casanova like me.

I encourage you to keep this book handy and refer to it often, until its principles for better sex, relationships and love become recurrent and customary for you. But, if you're seeking descriptions of what sexual organs are, how they look and function, statistical data with charts, pictures and graphs from major medical associations, university studies by doctors who never have sex, or the sexual advise of celibate priests, this is not the book for you.

However, if you already know what a penis is, what a vagina is, what an ass is, what breasts are, how they look and how they work, and you just want a simple guide to make you aware of certain things to avoid and other things that can make your sex life much better, then this is *exactly* the book for you. Our goal is to make having great sex no more complicated than it need be. With a little effort, everyone can have great sex and become a better lover—even you!

To everyone reading this book, I want you to know and believe that without a doubt you are beautiful. I am certain of this because, "There is beauty in everything but cannot be seen by everyone." So no matter how you look, don't worry, there's a special person just waiting to be discovered by you. This book is written knowing that you will find that special someone who sees the beauty in you. When you do find each other, with the information found on these pages you'll know precisely what to do to please him or her. I promise you, if you follow these few simple and easy steps, you will have a more pleasure-filled relationship and a much more enjoyable love and sex life…. I stake my reputation as a great lover on it!

Roberto Casanova

Extra Sensory Perception

*How is it that I can **Feel***
The rhythm of your heartbeat
from so very far across the world?
*How is it that I can **See***
The sparkle in your eyes shining so bright
even in complete darkness?
*How is it that I can **Hear***
The melody of your thoughts
even though we are miles and miles apart?
*How is it that I can **Taste***
The sweetness of your love even when my mouth is wide shut?
*How is it that I can **Smell***
The fragrance of your spirit
even as we stand in the midst of a rose garden?
…Maybe it's because
*I **Sense** myself falling in love with you…*

R. Ray Barnes

Making Love: Physical or Mental?

Battle of the sexes…

"We fuss, we fight, we kiss, we make up…"

Introduction Take II

Having Sex: Men vs. Women

In the July 12th, 2004 issue of *Newsweek*, in the article, *The Secret Lives of Wives*, by Lorraine Ali and Lisa Miller, it starts like this: "When groups of women get together, especially if they're mothers and have been married for more than six or seven years, and especially if there's alcohol involved, the conversation is usually the same. They talk about the kids and work—how stressed they are, how busy and bone tired. They gripe about their husbands and, if they're being perfectly honest and the wine kicks in, they talk about the disappointments in their marriages. Not long ago, over lunch in Los Angeles, this conversation took a surprising turn, when Erin, who

---

Men vs. Women

Men:
Tend to be lazy and follow the line of least resistance
Women:
Tend to resist following any line....

R. Ray Barnes

is in her early 40s and has been married for more than a decade, spilled it. She was seeing someone else. Actually, more than one person."

Later in the same article it states, "Just how many married women have had sex with people who are not their husbands? It's hard to say for sure, because people lie to pollsters when they talk about sex, and studies vary wildly. (Men, not surprisingly, amplify their sexual experience, while women diminish it.) Couples therapists estimate that among their clientele, the number is close to 30 to 40 percent, compared with 50 percent of men, and the gap is almost certainly closing."

Under the heading of the Sexual Habits Of American Women, *The Big Black Book*, published by Boardroom Classics, compiled a list of several magazine surveys regarding extramarital affairs and read as follows, "In a *Cosmopolitan* poll, 54% said they fooled around, 21% in a poll conducted by *Ladies' Home Journal*, 34% in *Playboy's*, and 43% in a survey by the *Institute for Advanced Study of Human Sexuality*. *Playboy's* poll also showed that almost 65% of wives have had affairs by age 50." Just think—with those being the statistics for women, it's frightening to imagine what they might be for men. Except, one statistic for women even made men look good by comparison. *Playboy* discovered that among young married couples, wives play around more than husbands do. My, how times have changed! Maybe the hunter is being captured by the game?

According to *DivorceGuide.com*, "Next to comparable countries, both the recent marriage rate and the annual divorce rate are higher in the United States." Moreover, they stated that approximately 60% of the American population is married, of which 50% of those marriages, (about 1 in 2) can be expected to end in divorce. Though marriage in America still seems to be *valued* deeply, U.S. Census data concurs, indicating a declining percentage of married adults: 54% in 2010, down from 57% in 2000 and 72% in 1960. In a Pew Research Center survey conducted in October of 2010, cohabitation has nearly doubled since 1990 (finding that 44% of adults have cohabited). And even more shocking, according to Pew, of the 2,691 adults who participated, 39% (four in ten) say marriage is becoming obsolete, up from 28% who responded to the same question posed by *Time* magazine in 1978.

The Hunted

I feel your arms around me and they feel so familiar
It's because they've been here before.
And as before, they are gone...
No one can explain this phenomenon,
No one has a reasonable explanation,
Does that sentence me to loneliness–one night stands?
I don't think so!
Just because my time clock runs faster
than most doesn't make it wrong.
Here's the challenge...
Open your mind and think for a moment.
Could it be I found you interesting enough to FUCK?
Could it be that that's MY idea of a first date?
Could it be that I'M horny too?
Or could it be you don't have the balls to deal?
*Could it be that a WOMAN is **easy***
but a MAN is conquering his prey!
SHIT! – Thought you knew! Women are HUNTERS too!
We walk in the night,
We study our prey,
We go in for the kill–
and BANG!!
Another trophy hangin' on our wall of fame–
Didn't know that did you?
*You were the **HUNTED***
***Not** the HUNTER!*

Leslie E. Pogue

As well, The State of Our Unions 2005, a report issued by the National Marriage Project at Rutgers University, indicated that only 63% of American children grow up with both biological parents—the lowest figure in the Western world.

In February 2007, the *Fox Cable News Channel* reported that 44% of adult Americans were single and there are more than 100 million unattached people in the United States. Like me, wouldn't you agree that something is very wrong with this picture? These statistics seem to suggest that our marriages and relationships have gone seriously awry. We need to discover a better way of getting along with each other, before we all go to hell in a hand basket.

Since most first marriages aren't lasting much longer than a successful TV sitcom, which according to *Divorce Magazine* is less than 8 years duration for both males and females, it may be prudent for first time couples or for those under the age of 25 to seek pre-marriage counseling to inform them of the challenges of marriage and to see if they are ready to make the necessary compromises and sacrifices it may take to have a successful marriage.

In light of the rapidly increasing divorce rate and reports that only 33% of married couples reach their 25th anniversary and only 5% their 50th, based on Divorce Magazine's data from 2002, maybe we should contemplate a new movement to change the Silver Anniversary from 25 to 10 years and the Golden Anniversary from 50 to 20 years, so as to not lose the celebration of them all together. Or, we could allow multiple marriages to qualify. If the length of time of all of your marriages adds up to 25 or 50 years respectively, then you may still celebrate your Silver and Gold Anniversaries. Something must be done. The trend seems to beg the question, "Is marriage becoming passé?" And, what role, if any, does good sex play in helping to maintain lasting marriages and relationships? Or, is good sex the cure-all?

In discussing the importance of sexual compatibility in marriages and relationships, to paraphrase Gideon Samid, author of *Try Again*, he intimated that when good sex was defined as consistent, lasting, intensive, pleasurable, satisfying, intimate and mutually exciting, most couples sited sexual compatibility as first and foremost in maintaining a successful marriage or relationship. Samid further proposed that, "If a couple enjoys good sex, as defined above, they will work out all other problems, and have a good marriage. If a couple does not enjoy good sex, then all sorts of problems (seemingly sexually unrelated), will pop up, and adversely impact the marriage."

Although sustaining a successful marriage is not quite as simple as just maintaining a good healthy sex life, sex does seem to play a major role. If there is *any* merit to Gideon Samid's ideas, and I believe there is, then couples learning to be more sexually compatible should be more likely to maintain better relationships and longer marriages.

According to Dr. Dean Edell, "Sex is really a family issue. Couples who enjoy great sex together are more likely to stay together. It is as simple as that."

However, in order to achieve sexual compatibility, one must be aware of his or her partner's sexual needs, wants and desires and how to satisfy them. This journey begins with understanding the mental, physical and sexual differences between men and women. With *69 Ways To Better Relationships, Sex and Love*, we do just that—help you to realize and appreciate those differences. So just sit back, relax and enjoy the ride, as we chauffeur you along to a more pleasurable relationship—with more fulfilling sex and a deep loving intimacy that will lead to better sexual compatibility.

There Are Vast Differences Between Men and Women

Although men and women may be part of the same human species, be mindful that they are not the same—men pee standing up and women pee sitting down; they both have breasts, but men's don't work; and while women can *have* babies, men often just *act* like babies. Plus, they don't look the same, think the same, feel the same, react the same, desire the same, nor do they expect the same. Men are from planet Mercury and women are from Pluto, or vice versa, depending on what day and time it is. As soon as one realizes, accepts and respects that there are vast differences between men and women, his or her potential for better sex, relationships and love will improve significantly. One's love life would be further enhanced, if he or she could learn to appreciate the differences between the sexes rather than despise them.

In the *Kundalini Research Institute International Teacher Training Manual Level 1*, under the heading, *Handling Female-Male Differences*, it suggests: "Study the nature of the male and female without judgment. Differences exist; they make life interesting and challenging. The male and female psyche each function in a very unique way, which causes each to perceive feelings, experiences, words, and even life very differently. When the male and the female do not recognize each other's unique gifts and challenges, misunderstandings and difficulties will occur."

According to Dr. Huntington F. Willard, Director of the Institute for Genome Sciences and Policy at Duke University, in a March, 2005 interview on the MSNBC Network show, *Connected Coast to Coast*, research involving the "X" chromosome, (females have 2 X chromosomes while males have one X and one Y) reveals that, "women are genetically more complex than men." Also, Dr. Nancy Snyderman, on the November 17, 2009 broadcast of her MSNBC show, *Dr. Nancy*, confirmed another interesting genetic difference in the sexes, saying that women are more likely than men to get addicted to tobacco, adding, "A woman's brain is different than a man's, true for tobacco and alcohol—much more sensitive, easier to get addicted, harder to quit."

Even though the full ramifications of the gene research are yet to be realized, it proves, once again, that not only are men and women different physically, emotionally and psychologically, but they are also very different genetically.

In addition, contemporary spiritual teacher and #1 New York Times Bestselling Author of *The Power Of Now*, Eckhart Tolle, in his book, *A New Earth*, says, "Although women have egos, of course, the ego can take root and grow more easily in the male form than in the female. This is because women are less mind-indentified than men. They are more in touch with the inner body and the intelligence of the organism where the intuitive faculties originate. The female form is less rigidly encapsulated than the male, has greater openness and sensitivity toward other life-forms, and is more attuned to the natural world."

Psychologist, Stephen Hamann, Ph.D., agrees that women and men are quite dissimilar. In an August 2005, broadcast of the popular Discovery Health Channel (DHC) TV show, *Strictly Sex With Dr. Drew*, Dr. Hamann asserted, "Women are a lot more complicated then men. It's sort of like a box that has one switch for the men and with women it's a box that has a hundred dials and different kinds of switches."

Another example illustrating the differences between men and women is how they perceive the common problem of jealousy. According to Rona Subotnik, marriage and family counselor, author of *Surviving Infidelity*, men and women are jealous for different reasons, "Women are more threatened by the physical attractiveness of other women... men, by the possibility that another man is a better lover. Women focus more on the emotional involvement of a spouse with someone else... men, on the sexual involvement."

One more very distinct disparity between men and women is a man's ability to totally disconnect emotionally from the act of making love and having sex, and a woman's innate ability to know in an instant upon meeting a potential male date, whether she would *ever* allow him the opportunity to sleep with her.

Most women need some kind of emotional spark or signal to trigger her ability to allow herself to make love to a man; even if she realizes that the sex may only be a one night stand. This sign she can determine almost immediately. Men require no such emotional spark, because given the chance, they'd like to sleep with almost any woman.

On the other hand, a woman needs to be *touched* by a man, or *feel* something *inside* that satisfies her emotionally enough to "make love" or even just to have sex with him.

This emotional spark or feeling seems to occur in most women despite the man's physical appearance. The man could be the most gorgeous hunk; however, if she doesn't feel that emotional spark or receive that *special* signal, she will in most cases not go through with it. If for some reason she does have sex or makes love to him having not felt that emotional spark, she often feels bad about it later. With most men, it's quite the contrary. Men have the ability to completely separate their emotions from the act of making love or having sex, without suffering any psychological consequence.

Most women have probably experienced an ex-lover approaching them about having sex again, (whether or not he or she is in a new relationship); he thinks it should be no big deal. For him it's simple—we know each other, we've done it several times before, so what's the problem? And even though she may be appalled, regarding his glib attitude toward them making love again, he doesn't get it, because he sincerely feels she should be able to simply disconnect her vagina from her heart, emotions and soul, just as he can with his penis. Damn, what can it hurt, he thinks, its *just sex*—we've done it a hundred times before. He thinks they should be able to *just do it*, walk away, effectively turning the whole event into a non-emotional, inconsequential act that he can't wait to do again. He can't even imagine how emotions should have anything to do with it; after all, to him, its *just sex*. It's really difficult for some men to understand that for a woman, it's almost *never* "just sex."

This "check and balance" system that we have with our attitudes toward sex and making love is quite necessary; so it mustn't be taken lightly. If women had the same, often superficial approach to making love and having sex as most men, it would be impossible for them to be the nurturers that they are and that we *need* them to be.

Women and men both need to recognize and understand and not be shocked or surprised, that in most cases a woman's first response to making love is emotional and a man's first response is physical.

Dr. Drew Pinsky, nationally renowned medical expert and host of *Strictly Sex, With Dr. Drew*, aptly stated, "For males it's the visual that activates the sex drive. Men seem to be more explicitly visual, while women take into account many more factors—I'll just go ahead and say it. Women are more evolved than us guys."

In a DHC *Strictly Sex Online Poll*, which posed the question, "What is the main force behind your sex drive?" The results were very telling. Male respondents said 70% was physical need, 20% emotional and 9% a need for romance. While women answered, 26% physical, 53% emotional and 11% a need for romance.

Another really very common occurrence illustrating how men and women are emotionally different is how women tend to react to the traumatic situations of their female friends. When two women get together to console one or the other, it can likely end with both of them hugging and in tears. However, in similar situations, men rarely or almost never end up literally crying on each other's shoulders.

Though it may not be as easy for men, if they would only *allow* themselves to be *touched* more emotionally, they'd be able to truly experience and comprehend all the wonderment (that women realize so easily) that "being in love" and "making love" has to offer.

To even further exemplify this disparity between the sexes and to have you *truly* appreciate what I mean by the "differences" in the way men and women think when it relates to having sex and making love, I like to use this hypothetical scenario.

If we solicited ten self-confessed happily married men and told them the following—that women the likes of Halle Berry, Catherine Zeta-Jones, Angelina Jolie, Jessica Alba, Beyonce Knowles, Kristin Davis, etc., were willing to do them a huge favor and have sex with them and allow the men to perform oral sex on them—with a guarantee that their wives would never find out about it—*most* of these ten happily married men would do it in a heartbeat, consider themselves lucky, and brag about it to their friends.

On the contrary, if we made the same offer to ten happily married women, with men the likes of Tom Cruise, Antonio Banderas, Brad Pitt, Denzel Washington, Sean Connery, Will Smith, et al., and told them that these men would do them a huge favor and have sex with them and allow the women to perform oral sex on them—*most* of these ten women would consider it an insult and would refuse on principle alone.

Most married men will profess upstanding moral behavior in the light of day, but will employ very few moral principles when they are faced with the chance of having hot steamy sex with a beautiful woman in the dark of night with a guarantee of not being caught. On the other hand, even though female infidelity is on the rise, I believe most married women do have principles when it comes to having sex and making love and in most cases, will exercise them. However, with men, at times such as these, whatever principles they do possess are usually tossed right out the window. Now you see, that's the difference! Most women make use of some principles when it comes to sex and most men don't.

You must understand, in most cases men want to make a sexual 'score' at any cost, married or not. At those critical times when men are confronted with an opportunity to score sexually with a beautiful woman, all reason is lost and abandoned and they see themselves as Kobe Bryant with one-second left to score to win the championship. Lord have mercy if he actually scores. If successful, he will then perceive his ejaculation of millions of sperm to be fans cheering him on and he will feel like the world's greatest superhero lover. After that, he convinces himself that he could save the whole of female humanity by rescuing every sex-starved woman, one at a time, or even the same sex-starved woman over and over again. If he makes it to this point, then his ability to reason is lost until he gets caught. Then, like "presto, change-o, ala-ka-zam," his reasoning capabilities magically reappear as he expresses sorrow for what he has done. Now, having lost his superhero status, with his most pitiful look he pleads, "Don't blame me, I'm *just* a man, God made me this way."

Though I know it may sound ridiculous, but to this end, men may just have a point. Men *are* at a distinct disadvantage. God cursed men by giving them two heads and therefore two necks. Consequently men try to think with both their heads and talk out of both their necks. Yet they've failed to realize that only one of their heads has been equipped with a brain. And because men have developed a reputation for taking the easy way out more times than not, they will allow the head without the brain to do most of their thinking.

I am in no way excusing men's behavior, or justifying or condoning it. It's just that in reality, men and women process and think differently regarding sex and making love. Until we recognize and accept these facts, we can't begin to deal with relationships more effectively. Understanding, accepting, and appreciating these differences about the sexes will be your first step toward a much better sex life.... If you don't, oh well, I guess I'll see you in therapy, divorce court, the crazy house, jail, or even worse—on Jerry Springer or Maury. But men, beware! A Chinese proverb says, "Man who fish in other man's fishing hole, often catch crab."

Now ladies, I know you're smiling now, but don't relax yet; you're not without blame. Many men feel when they think of a wo*man* that it really means "*woe-is-man.*" On the contrary, I know that when some women just see the words *Men*strual cramps, *Men*opause, *Men*tal illness, *Men*tal breakdown, *Men*tal cruelty, *Men*tal abuse and *Men*ace to society, they can become easily convinced that men are the source of all of their pain. In addition, when women are really having major problems it requires a *His*terectomy by a *Guy*necologist (poetic spelling of course). Even though there's some merit to the idea that men may be the cause of a many a woman's grief and anguish, women also, by their own actions, promote certain behaviors in men.

For instance, when your teenage boys start dating and you find that they only like one girl, you encourage them to date many others at the same time. I know you do it to protect him, not wanting him to be smitten before he's old enough to handle it. But, unless you make perfectly clear why you're advocating he date others, he gets the message (from his mother, no less), that it's okay to date more than one girl at a time. And ladies, many men claim that dating multiple women is a very difficult habit to break. They compared it to cigarettes or even heroin; and they blame you for it. Men notice right away—if they want to get attention from beautiful women, all they need do is be seen escorting other beautiful women. It seems clear that many women are attracted to men who are always seen dating other beautiful women. Okay ladies, now explain that, given that you're always harping on men about fidelity.

Furthermore, what is it about a man that is such a turn-on for a woman when he's seen alone with a young child or a baby? It's fairly likely that he may be in a relationship, seeing that the child is so young.

But women seem to flock to men under such circumstances. Men are known to receive much more attention or "action" from women when they are seen alone with babies or small children.

And what about those women who tell their best girlfriends in confidence about how *super* a lover their man is in bed—only to find themselves betrayed by their trusted girlfriends who have decided to be rescued by their best friend's superhero lover?

It's easy to understand how a woman may want to be with that man who is always seen with beautiful women—figuring that he must be a "good catch" if *so* many beautiful women are interested in spending time with him. And what woman would not want to be with that seemingly kind and loving gentleman we witness alone taking care of a baby or small child? Also, I think all ladies would agree that they'd like to be with a man who is a great lover in bed. But at what cost to womanhood do women pay to exercise those desires?

So, needless to say, both sexes could use a little work. Though, I think most would agree that men are generally perceived to be the first to begin misbehaving, they still need a female accomplice to complete their dastardly deeds. I think there's enough blame to pass around—I invite he or she who has not sinned to cast the first stone.... With no stones cast, let's take a journey and explore some of the things we can *all* do—with 69 Ways To Better Relationships, Sex and Love—with 43 poems, photographs and a few laughs—to make relationships and lovemaking better for both sexes

Julie Lovelace

A Special Note...

With all that we've stated thus far, one of the most despairing differences between the sexes is gender inequality as it relates to basic health care. *Time.com* noted, "According to a report released on Nov. 9 (2009) by the World Health Organization, millions of women die each year from conditions that could be avoided — if they were men. Apart from hazards like female infanticide and maternal deaths, women are more likely to contract HIV, suffer from depression and domestic abuse, and lack access to basic health care that could help them survive."

Having Sex: Men vs. Women

"Remember to take time to smell your flowers…"

"Be playful, silly and laugh sometimes…"

Introduction Take III

The Rate-A-Date Scale

Before we unveil these 69 Ways To Better Relationships, Sex and Love, as the title implies, we must first devise a better method for accurately assessing the mates and potential dates you currently have or may encounter in the near future.

In America, and as a world society, we have become obsessed with ratings and surveys involving everything we do. Whether it's the *AC Nielsen Ratings*, telling us which TV and Radio shows are the best, or *J.D. Power and Associates* telling us which automobiles performed the best in a variety of categories (including frontal and side impact crash test), we are bombarded with ratings and surveys. It's truly great to know how safe a car is, but if it lacks good styling I doubt that you would buy it. Most would prefer a safe car that also has attractive styling.

We almost all utilize the now accepted uniform "5 Star System," for rating hotels and vacation resorts. Each hotel or resort is awarded 1 to 5 stars to indicate how luxurious or "nice" it is, with the identical number of stars being comparatively equivalent to the same level of quality regardless of the brand name of the hotel. The hotel quality increases based on the number of stars awarded it. The system is handy and helpful, but doesn't always account for things that may be important to us other than the overall quality of the hotel. Sometimes a 3 Star hotel that's closer to the places we plan to patronize may be much more preferable than a 5 Star hotel several miles away. You see, most prefer convenience along with a degree of luxury.

Not only do we rate hotels, cars, household appliances, electronic devices and almost anything else known to man with the likes of *Consumer Reports, J.D. Power, ACNielsen*, but rating the products and services we use everyday has become a multi-billion dollar industry. Every major news organization now has substantial polling operations. From macho sports shows to the late night talk show host, everyone has one's own "Top Ten List" for something. In our society, we have a burning desire and a desperate need to know who or what rates *good, better,* or *best*.

Since 1979 when the Bo Derek, Dudley Moore and Julie Andrews movie, *10* topped the box office, we've been assigning each other a rating number on how "good looking" we are and how much "sex appeal" we have. We do it with everyone. Whether it's our husband, wife, lover, mate, date, neighbor or the girl or guy who delivers the mail in the office building where we work. We're obsessed with it. Of course, we do it with the idea that the closer one rates to a "10," the better looking this individual is and the more sex appeal he or she possesses.

Many of us have used the '10' rating scale system to choose our own dates and to match-up likely dating candidates for our friends. Most of the time these matches end in disaster, because the '10' dating scale is inherently flawed. It only includes half of the equation—physical appeal. It may indicate how good someone looks, but says nothing about one's personality and intellect. Thus, you sometimes end up with a great looker, who is brain dead and has the personality of a possum or an alligator. Needless to say, a new scale is required and is much overdue, one that incorporates the most important missing part of the equation—mental and personal appeal. And we have endeavored to do just that with the creation of the *"10 Heart"* Rate-A-Date Scale *("RAD Scale")*.

The Rate-A-Date Scale

With the *RAD Scale* you get to quickly rate your date with qualities important to you, both physically and mentally. The *RAD Scale* is easy, because it uses the same basic guidelines, which are already familiar to you. As with the 5 Star ratings for hotels, with the *RAD Scale* you award a maximum of "5 Hearts" for someone's combined "Sexuality and Good Looks," and an additional maximum of "5 Hearts" for his or her "Personality and Intellect." Once having assessed one's qualities in these two linked-together areas, the totals are now combined into a more accurate *10 Heart RAD Scale* to determine whether one is a *"true"* 10 or not. This gives you the opportunity to a make a much better assessment of the desirability of a would-be date and its likelihood of any long-term potential.

Listed on *The RAD Scale Questions Chart* below are a few helpful questions you might want to ask yourself in evaluating prospective dates. It suggests questions regarding both physical and mental appeal. To achieve the best results, it's better to be completely honest with yourself when making your evaluations. Questions require a simple yes, no or maybe so. "Yes," meaning it's something that you really love about them. "No," meaning it's something that doesn't quite appeal to your particular taste, and "Maybe so," meaning that it's acceptable, not necessarily good or bad.

The answers to any of the questions, all very subjective, are only meant to serve as a guideline. Each individual will ultimately have to decide the weight of each date's qualities and come to his or her own conclusions. Even so, the *10 Heart Rate-A-Date Scale* is quite telling and shouldn't be taken lightly—although it should be lots of fun.

The RAD Scale Questions Chart

Questions to consider when you are evaluating prospective dates.

Physical Appeal	Mental Appeal
Sexuality & Good Looks	**Personality & Intellect**
1. Is the Face Appealing?	1. Are you Comfortable together?
2. Is the Body Shape Appealing?	2. Do you Communicate well?
3. Do you like the Smile?	3. Is he/she Fun to be with?
4. Do you like the Eyes?	4. Do you like his/her sense of Humor?
5. Do you like the Hair?	5. Is he/she Honest and Trustworthy?
6. Do you like the Height?	6. Is he/she Kind and Considerate?
7. Is he/she Well Groomed?	7. Is there Mutual Respect?
8. Do you like the Speaking Voice?	8. Do you share Goals and Desires?
9. Does he/she Smell Good?	9. Is he/she Knowledgeable?
10. Do you like how he/she Dresses?	10. Is he/she Smart and Intelligent?
11. Do you like one's Hands & Feet?	11. Do you like how he/she Thinks?
12. Is he/she Sexually Appealing?	12. Are you Spiritually in tune?
13. Do you or could you like how he/she looks when Waking Up?	13. Is he/she free from Destructive and Addictive Behaviors?

Now that you've answered some key questions regarding your date, check *The RAD Scale Heart Chart* below to see how to rate your date's qualities. Each 'yes' answer is awarded **1** heart, a 'maybe so' answer is awarded a **0.5** heart, and no hearts are awarded for a 'no' answer.

For example, if your answers total 11 to 12.5 on Physical Appeal, you award your prospective date 4 hearts. If your answers total 8 to 10.5 regarding their Mental Appeal, you award them 3 hearts, as indicated on the chart. You then combine the 4 hearts plus 3, and your date would rate a 7 on the *RAD Scale*.

The RAD Scale Heart Chart

Physical Appeal Questions Answered Yes		Mental Appeal Questions Answered Yes	
Number Range	Award	Number Range	Award
13	5 Hearts	13	5 Hearts
11 to 12.5	4 Hearts	11 to 12.5	4 Hearts
8 to 10.5	3 Hearts	8 to 10.5	3 Hearts
4 to 7.5	2 Hearts	4 to 7.5	2 Hearts
1 to 3.5	1 Heart	1 to 3.5	1 Heart

Now that you know how to rate your date on the *RAD Scale*, what does it all mean? Well, look no further; we will decipher your results for you in the following list, *How Your Date Rates On The RAD Scale*. However, we remind and warn you that some of our lighthearted suggestions may be a tad bit over the top—you are responsible for making the final determinations for evaluating your potential dates. Have fun and enjoy the process.

How Your Date Rates On The RAD Scale

Total Hearts	Correspond the total number of hearts given to your mate to see how he or she rates.
0 to 0.5	You can't miss what you can't measure. And remember, nothing from nothing leaves nothing.
1 to 1.5	Houston, we have a problem…Just check his or her pulse and call 911 Emergency.
2 to 2.5	Drop it like it's hot! This date may be a Jerry Springer reject, so I wouldn't touch this one with a ten-foot pole.
3 to 3.5	Kiss and don't tell anyone! Reserve this date for when you're drunk and for booty calls only.

4 to 4.5	Sometimes you feel like a nut, sometimes you don't. You might want it, but do you really need it? So have a fresh set of batteries or plenty of Vaseline and maybe some Tylenol, too.
5 to 5.5	You might just want to try it out for size. And if it doesn't fit, don't force it.... Don't try to fit a square peg into a round hole. It may be better to just hit it and quit it.
6 to 6.5	Try it, you might like it.... But just know, it might be like Chinese food—satisfying for the moment, but won't fill you up.
7 to 7.5	When you roll the dice in Las Vegas, 7 is a winner—so take a chance and go for it... You might get lucky—and if you do, just do it 'til you're satisfied or until you roll craps.
8 to 8.5	8's Great! Dive right in—feet, head or heart first, it's up to you. But if you study long, you study wrong; so like Nike says, Just Do It! Just remember, still waters run deep.
9 to 9.5	Caution: This love is hot! So don't wait, don't hesitate, just put the pedal to the metal. When opportunity knocks, open the door and let 'em in! In other words, "If the shoe fits, wear it."
10	One in a million! A perfect combination! So go ahead, climb this stairway to heaven and when you get there don't be surprised to find that you may have found your soul mate. Don't order the ring yet, but find out the size.

Now that you have mastered how to rate your dates using the *RAD Scale*, we have supplied for you a convenient *Rate-A-Date Comparison Chart* so that you can easily discover at a glance the most desirable date for you—then you can put to use all of the *69 Ways To Better Relationships, Sex and Love*.

Rate-A-Date Comparison Chart

Name of Date	Physical Hearts	Mental Hearts	Total Hearts
1.			
2.			
3.			
4.			
5.			

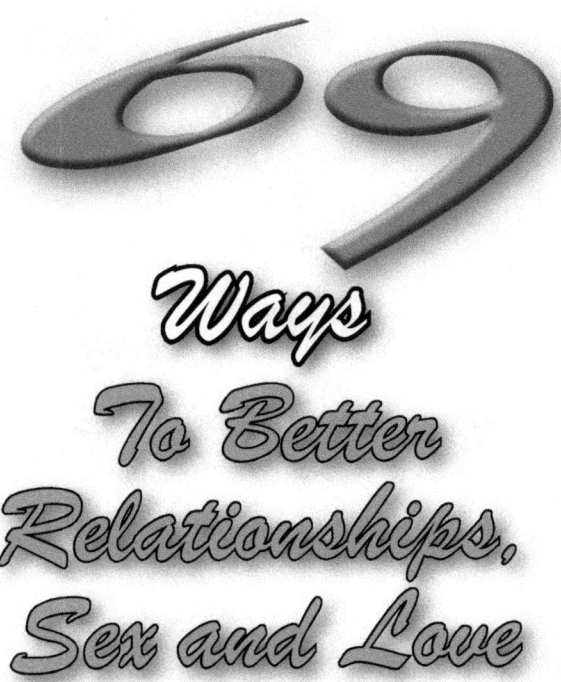

69 Ways
To Better Relationships, Sex and Love

"Study the Love Rules of the Road together…"

Chapter One

Love Rules of the Road

Before we begin, as with any journey we must obey the rules of the road—with relationships it's no different. After making your decision to travel along the highway of relationships, sex and love, be sure to keep in mind the following love rules of the road. A humorous look....

***1.* Check The 'Whether' Conditions:** Before setting off on your journey to Erotic City, in the State of Orgasmic Bliss, it may do you both well to check the *whether* conditions. Guys, try to discern *whether* your chances are sunny, partly cloudy, rainy, stormy or otherwise. If you know *whether* you'll have good road conditions, it will allow you to better prepare for your journey ahead, helping you to avoid potholes, floods, unexpected detours and road closures that may lie before you.

After you cum...

After you "cum," do you know where you are going?

R. Ray Barnes

Although it's not always possible, ladies, know ahead of time *whether* you intend to let him drive your vehicle or not. And to avoid personal injury, make sure you know *whether* he has a clean driving record before you allow him to get behind your wheel. Guys, know the body style and type of vehicle she has before, "getting inside" to drive. You'll want to know *whether* you need to work a stick, if it's automatic or just set on cruise control? Furthermore, you should always carry the proper safety, liability and child accident insurance.

Knowing the *whether* conditions will save you both a great deal of trepidation, when and if the time 'comes' for you to ride into Erotic City, in the State of Orgasmic Bliss together.

2. Don't Forget Your Safety and Emergency First Aid Kit: Remember to protect yourself at all times. Bring plenty of packs of condoms, lubricant, massage oils, gels, whipped cream, chocolate syrup, ice cubes, (peanut butter) and K-Y Jelly, etc. And always carry an air pump with you in case your tire goes flat and you have to jack it up. Also, be sure to have a big screwdriver on hand so you can loosen a screw as well as tighten a screw. Plus, have a large hammer, so if by chance you have to nail it, you'll be prepared. The last thing you want is to have a breakdown right outside Erotic City and be unable to fix it. And by the way, AAA doesn't respond to sexual emergencies—so always 'come' prepared—because accidents can and do happen!

A. Healthful Hints: STDs

In today's age and times, when thinking of having sex, one must think of safety first. Sexually Transmitted Diseases, commonly known as STDs, are on the rise and are becoming increasingly dangerous.

According to our physician consultant, Karen M. Webster, M.D., MPH, "In the year 2010, there really isn't anything sexy about having sex without a condom. This is because there is nothing sexy about contracting HIV (human immunodeficiency virus), syphilis, herpes, human papilloma virus (HPV), gonorrhea, Chlamydia, or hepatitis B, which are some of the most common sexually transmitted infections.

These diseases are all still alive and well and unfortunately continue to play a role in loss of life, loss of fertility, cervical cancer, liver disease as well as simple pain and suffering. Our bodies are our temples and until we are sure that we are in a mutually monogamous relationship with someone who has been tested for all of the above, our best protection is the consistent and correct use of a latex condom.

Sadly, infection from HIV is increasing at an alarming rate, especially amongst heterosexual women (women who have sex with men) and those who are poor. You never want to wake up the morning after, wondering whether the night before might change your health and your life forever."

The American Social Health Association advises that you should be tested once a year even if you are feeling fine. They also suggest that if you are experiencing any of the following symptoms you should go to the doctor or visit a clinic right away. 1). Pain when you go to the bathroom. 2). A strange fluid or drip from the penis or the vagina. 3). Bleeding between periods (women).

Dr. Webster reminds us that as many as 60% of women who are diagnosed with Chlamydia may have no symptoms at all. So testing is especially important for women under the age of 25, particularly those who have had three or more sexual partners in their lifetime.

To find out where you can get free testing and treatment in your area, call the CDC National STD Hotline at 1-800-227-8922. There are also sites where your testing can be completely anonymous, (without your legal name or any identifying information associated with the test).

For more information regarding STDs, we encourage you to visit the CDC National Prevention Information Network's website at www.cdcnpin.org, and the American Social Health Association's website, at www.ashastd.org.

*Healthful Hints are for information only;
for medical advice see a doctor.*

3. **Have a Trip Plan:** It's good to know where you are going and the roads you plan to travel to get there. You will want to know if the roads are going to be smooth, rough, wet or dry. Certainly you will want to be cognizant of the size of your gas tank, the price of gas and how many miles your vehicle gets to the gallon. On this kind of pleasure trip you surely don't want to run out of gas.

Ladies, if you intend to entice him and wear something sexy before he hits the road and starts to drive, be ready; timing is of the essence, and you don't want to delay the send off.... Furthermore guys, don't try to play with her gearbox, after you've just finished flushing the radiator and you've got coolant and grease all over your hands. Her gears are very sensitive, so make sure your hands are clean at all times.

This doesn't mean you can't be spontaneous and make a couple stops and take in the sights along the way. However, at least know whether you're going north to Alaska in the winter when it's very cold and windy, or south to Florida in the summer when it's extremely hot and humid. You will find that certain *whether* conditions will require a different mindset and preparations. Moreover, as mentioned before, "After you 'cum,' know where you are going."

4. **Fasten Your Seatbelts:** You may be in for a rough ride, it all depends on the road conditions and the type of vehicle your lover drives—whether it makes 2 strokes or 4, whether the crankshaft pushes the pistons into a weak 4 cylinder head or into a powerful 12, and whether it's a meager 2-wheel drive or a rugged off-road 4 wheeler.

It also matters what kind of driver one is—whether one likes to arrive premature and early, take it slow and easy, or drive the freeways switching lanes trying to get a-'head'. (Now that would be cunnilingus or fellatio for some of you). But, no matter the driver, just remember, "When the going gets tough, the tough get going."

5. **Adjust Your Mirrors:** You need to be aware of everything around you, so keep your lover in view. It's a must that you know where all your lover's sensual parts are at all times. You don't want to make the mistake of smacking her breast and licking her butt (annilingus or "rimming" for some of you). Although, who knows, some of you might; so at least know where everything is.

6. **Obey the Speed Limit:** Guys, watch your speed. Be aware of sudden hairpin turns, bumps in the road and unexpected detours. In most cases it's better to let her set the speed limit. However, be sure to keep pace; don't lag too far behind and almost never pass her. Remember, she's the traffic cop, the judge and the jury. She has the power to write you a ticket, suspend your license, impound your vehicle, put you in sexual jail and revoke your bail.

7. **Learn to Yield:** Guys it will do you good to learn to yield to *her* wants and desires. Although you may be driving the limousine, she's the passenger and it's your job to take her wherever she wants to go. In other words, when it comes to sex and making love, learn to give-in and yield to what she wishes and prefers. And, if you yield without a fight, if she cares for you, I guarantee she'll give you the "Right of Way" later.

You must be very careful when you neglect to fulfill her wishes, because sometimes her requests are just a test to see how much you're willing to give or bend. This way, she's able to discern how selfish you are, as well as whether you're trustworthy and deserving enough for her to fulfill *your* wants and desires. But by *no means* do you try to fool her; her woman's intuition will catch you! Be honest! If you truly feel you shouldn't submit to her, then don't. She will feel that honest rejection is better than deceitful acquiescence. And though you may think her tactics a bit unfair, don't be angry with her; she's at much greater risk than you and has a lot more to lose.

Moreover, guys, don't allow your egos to make you think that by giving in to her you're losing control; you're not. Women view strength and control differently than men. She sees your ability to yield at the *proper* time as a "strength"—so in reality, in her eyes, you're not losing control; you're gaining it. The lesson here is for you to *think first*, before you let your ego think for you, and don't let her (very easy to satisfy) minor requests become (very difficult to solve) major problems.

8. Watch for Turn Signals, U-Turns and Backup Lights: Guys, after you've yielded to her wants and desires, watch for any other signals she may be giving. Women have been known to make unexpected U-turns, back up in the middle of the road, turn left, or put up a roadblock just as you're about to enter her intersection. So be prepared to stop on a dime and change directions without getting angry. There should be no "road rage" on Love Street. Always be sweet as well as understanding, keeping in mind that you attract more bees with honey than with vinegar. But be cautious; bees like honey, but if aggravated, they will sting.

Blinking Constantly...

*I think about you often—
for no particular reason, but for many reasons…
reasons for which I don't quite understand…yet.
when sleeping—there you are,
when awaking—there you are,
when coming—there you are,
when going—there you are,
when arriving—there you are,
when I've already left before I even knew I was there—
there you are.
I carry an image of you in my minds' eye
and look at it often—
it's as if your beautiful smile is attached
to the insides of my eyelids
and every time I close my eyes—there you are!
I now find myself Blinking Constantly and smiling…*

R. Ray Barnes

***9.* It's Slippery When Wet:** Guys, if it's not wet, it means not yet. Like the Chinese proverb says, "If don't fit, you mus-a-quit." Never complain about a woman not being wet or lubricated, because if she's not, in most cases, it may be your fault. You're probably not making her feel relaxed or comfortable enough. So like Mr. Goodwrench, always carry your toolbox with you and keep handy a good supply of water-based lubricants. If you want her to let you use *your* dipstick, at least you could supply the oil. Plus, if you've got the right apparatus to tighten her screw, she just might let you put a nut on it.

So, if she happens to be a little dry, take the few extra seconds to apply some lubricant. I guarantee it will be well worth the extra minutes or hours of uninterrupted pleasure that it may provide. And ladies, don't be too shy or embarrassed to bring to his attention before intercourse, that you may need additional lubrication, it's often very difficult for men to tell, and it's nothing to feel bad about or to be ashamed to mention.

B. Healthful Hints: Vaginal Dryness

According to the MayoClinic.com, "Vaginal dryness is a common condition that affects women of all ages. It's estimated that 10 percent to 40 percent of women who've reached menopause have symptoms related to vaginal dryness."

They also state that when your vagina isn't properly lubricated, it can feel itchy and irritated, making sexual intercourse less pleasurable.

Occasional vaginal dryness during intercourse may mean that you aren't sufficiently aroused. For those times, increased foreplay with your partner may help you to become aroused and lubricated.

Karen M. Webster, M.D., MPH, says, "Although vaginal dryness is often due to lack of, or inadequate stimulation, a woman's decreasing stores of the female hormone estrogen can also cause it.

> *As women age and particularly as they go through or come close to going through menopause, estrogen levels decrease and the vaginal mucosa (surface) may be less moist. So what may have been enough stimulation earlier in life may not produce the same response later in life—its just part of our natural maturation cycle. Water-based lubricants and tenderness are still the right answer. However, in some cases, if the dryness is persistent and causes too much discomfort, estrogen creams may be needed and prescribed by a doctor."*
>
> *The Mayo Clinic also recommends some over-the-counter water-based lubricants such as Astroglide and K-Y Liquid to relieve some of the discomfort associated with vaginal dryness. There are many medical causes for vaginal dryness, and for any prolonged pain and discomfort you should see a doctor.*
>
> *However, when you are experiencing bouts of vaginal dryness during sexual intercourse the Mayo Clinic says, "Avoid using these products to treat vaginal dryness as they may irritate your vagina: Vinegar, yogurt or other douches, hand lotions, soaps (and) bubble baths."*
>
> *For more information on vaginal dryness we encourage you to visit the Mayo Clinic's website, at www.MayoClinic.com.*

*Healthful Hints are for information only;
for medical advice see a doctor.*

10. Obey the Traffic Signal Lights: The *Red Light* means to *STOP!* So ladies, when you say STOP, you should really mean for him to STOP! Don't tell him to stop as a way to convey that you're not being too easy, when you really want him to continue. You should always, as they say, "Say what you mean and mean what you say." Sometimes it's very confusing for men when you're saying, "STOP," while ripping his clothes off and yours at the same time. However, we recommend in today's age and time that it's best for all men to assume that *anything* a woman says that sounds even close to "No,"

"Don't," "I don't know," "I don't think so," "I'm not sure," or "STOP" should be taken as a *Red Light* and means you should really STOP! If you have any doubts, just ask Mike Tyson or Kobe Bryant or anyone confronted with claims of sexual assault.

The Yellow Light means to proceed with CAUTION. When she's indicating or saying anything but a resounding YES, always make it a habit to proceed with CAUTION!

The Green Light means it's okay to proceed or GO. At which point, you should quickly proceed before she decides to make a U-turn, back up, turn left or put up a roadblock. However, if you both obey the *Loves Rules of the Road*, you'll have a safe trip and a more pleasurable ride!

Infinite Voyage

our **Love** is like the universe
...it's forever exp a n d i **n** g
our **Love** is like a shooting star
...it's never
l
a
n
d
i
n
g
but,
our **Journey**
is not without a destination...
for every moment reveals
A New Place...
every thought unveils
A New Port...

> *and every touch gives way to*
> *A New Discovery...*
> *our **Love** is an*
> *INFINITE VOYAGE...*
> *through*
> *Love & Spirit, Mind & Body,*
> *Heart & Soul, Time & Space...*
> *and oh what a*
> *Wonderful Ride!*
>
> *R. Ray Barnes*

"Yes! We're gonna do just what the book says..."

Chapter Two

Licking the Myths

To properly prepare you for your journey, there is some "myth information" we need to discuss, regarding relationships, sex and making love. Many people have been misguided by myths, and as a consequence, caused problems in their relationships. One must be careful not to give too much weight to unsubstantiated rumors and punning tales.... Sometimes, just a little simple logic and common sense will do the trick.

If life is about what Is…

*If Life is about **Is**, why do we worry so much about what **Ain't**?*

R. Ray Barnes

---

11. Size Does Matter… Right? Penis size does matter, if you've got size; it doesn't matter, if you don't. Remember, "It's not the size of the ship that makes you sea sick, it's just the motion of the ocean." According to Alex Comfort, M. B., D.Sc., author of *The New Joy of Sex*, he says, "Preoccupation with the size of one's genitals is as built-in biologically to men (it is a 'dominance signal,' like a deer's antlers) as sensitivity about one's breasts and figure is to women. That, however, is its only importance. The 'average' size penis is about six inches overall when erect and about 3-1/2 inches round, but penises come in all sizes—larger ones are spectacular but no more effective except as visual stimuli. Smaller ones work equally well in most positions." Comfort adds, "Non-erect size in the male is equally unimportant."

Some men have size but don't know what to do with it, thinking that their size is all they need. While others have size but are much too big for the average woman (8 inches or more) and never really get to use all they have; and that can be miserable. So having a huge size penis is not always a blessing for a guy.

On the other hand, there are average size guys who, like the old slogan for Avis Rent A Car, simply "try harder" at pleasing their lover. These average-size guys tend to employ other methods to satisfy their lovers; not just relying on their penis size. Because of the extra effort, in many cases the "average-size" guys prove much better lovers than their oversized counterparts. So size isn't everything. But *pleasing* her is. With some women, however, size does matter. Some prefer to have a man with a large penis, if he's not *too* big and knows how to use what he's got. Otherwise, bigger is not always better; sometimes it's *just* bigger. We also discovered, that the *bigger* issue for most women was the *smaller* issue—a penis that's too small. Almost all agreed that an extremely small penis wasn't very desirable. So maybe size does matter after all—not how big, but how small.

C. Healthful Hints: Prostate Health

Rather than being so concerned about the size of one's apparatus, men would be better served being concerned about the size of one's prostate.

An enlarged prostate can affect a man's sexual performance and desire. According to Prostate.com, "As men age, the prostate may become a source of problems."

According to Dr. Webster, the prostate gland is a walnut sized gland that makes the fluid that forms semen. As men age, the gland increases in size and can cause the urethra (the tube that carries urine from the bladder, where it collects, through the penis to outside of the body) to narrow. This is called benign prostatic hypertrophy (BPH) and may cause symptoms such as difficulty starting the urinary stream, frequent urination and nocturia (urinating excessively at night). Your doctor, who may treat them with oral medications, should evaluate these symptoms.

Cancer cells may also form within the prostate gland. In fact, prostate cancer is the most commonly diagnosed cancer in men in the United States. (2nd only to skin cancer in rates of diagnosis and 2nd only to lung cancer in cancer related deaths in American men). It is estimated that 200,000 new cases will be diagnosed this year and as many as 40,000 men will die of prostate cancer.

The screening guidelines for prostate cancer vary. The American Urological Association recommends routine yearly screening for males at average risk beginning at age 50 with a digital rectal exam (where a medical professional inserts a gloved finger into the rectum to feel the prostate gland in order to assess size and other abnormalities), and a blood test for a tumor marker called PSA. The American Cancer Society recommends these tests be offered annually to men, who are age 50 or older, and who are expected to live at least another 10 years (for example, have no other potentially life threatening or serious chronic illnesses). Men in certain high-risk groups, namely African American men and those who have a family history of prostate cancer in a father or brother, should begin screening at age 40-45.

The symptoms of prostate cancer and BPH may be similar and include difficulty with urination, weak or interrupted urine flow, excessive urination at nighttime, blood in urine or semen, or pain with urination. Any of these symptoms should prompt a visit to your doctor for further evaluation.

> *According to bodyandfitness.com, maintaining a healthy prostate can be more fun than you think; it says, "Ejaculating regularly through sex can reduce the risk of prostate cancer. So lady—if you care about the health of your man's prostate, you know what you need to do."*
>
> *For more information on maintaining good prostate health and awareness, we encourage you to visit, www.Prostate.com, www.UrologyHealth.org from the American Urological Association, and the American Cancer Society website, www.cancer.org.*

Healthful Hints are for information only;
for medical advice see a doctor.

12. Big Hands, Big Feet, Big D...? People have often wondered about the myth suggesting that one can tell the size of a man's penis based on the size of his hands, feet, and body. Following that logic, if this myth were true, then professional basketball star Shaquille O'Neal would be the size of a horse and "Mini-Me" (from the movie *Austin Powers*) would need tweezers; yet, the myth is alive and well.

In *SEX: A Man's Guide*, a Canadian study, which sized up 63 men's penises is quoted, "They measured their height and shoe sizes to see if there's any truth to the folklore that you can estimate a man's overall body size or the size of his feet. The doctors found only the weakest of correlations." However, another commonly purported myth associated with penis size seems to be true. Sex expert and author Tracey Cox, stated on the *Oprah Show* on June 2, 2005, that, "Research confirms that Asian men are the smallest, followed by Caucasians, with African-American men definitely being the largest."

However, putting all the myths and research aside, many women feel that no matter the size of their hands and feet, men are just like snow storms–you never know when they're coming, how many inches you will get, or how long they will last.

13. **Breast Size... The Bigger the Better?** Some people have mistakenly assumed that a woman's breast size has some correlation with her sensitivity and sex drive. Not so, as indicated by Judith Seifer, R.N., Ph.D., President of the American Association of Sex Educators, Counselors and Therapists, who said that the size of a woman's breasts has no more to do with a woman's sex drive than the size of a man's penis has to do with a man's sex drive. Other experts also concur that breast size has nothing to do with breast sensitivity. As per Jolan Chang, writing in *The Tao of Love and Sex*, a book about ancient Chinese sexual techniques, "Strange as it may seem, the size or beauty of a woman's breast is irrelevant to whether she enjoys them being kissed, sucked, or licked." But he adds: "With many women there is a connection between nipples and vulva. Stimulating these two delicate buttons either by kissing, sucking or caressing will... quickly result in the vagina overflowing with lubricant."

Kissing a woman's breast, according to *SEX: A Man's Guide*, is, "... One of men's absolute favorite sexual daydreams." In fact, in one University of Missouri study of male sex fantasies, kissing a pair of monumental breasts was the second-most frequently mentioned fantasy (outranked only by the thought of getting turned on by a pair of terrific legs). The really interesting news is that when women in the same study were asked their favorite fantasies, the one they mentioned most often was... having a man kiss their breasts."

D. *Healthful Hints: Breast Examinations*

Men from time immemorial have admired women's breasts, yet they do carry with them their own set of problems.

According to the American Cancer Society (ACS), "Breast cancer is the most common cancer among women, other than skin cancer. It is the second leading cause of cancer death in women, after lung cancer. About 207,000 women in the United States will be found to have invasive breast cancer in 2010. About 40,000 women will die from the disease this year. Right now there are slightly over two million women living in the U.S. who have been treated for breast cancer. The chance of a woman having invasive breast cancer some time during her life is about 1 in 8. The chance of dying from breast cancer is about 1 in 35. Breast cancer death rates are going down. This decline is probably the result of earlier detection and improved treatment." The ACS recommends the following guidelines for finding breast cancer early in women without symptoms: Mammogram: *Women age 40 and older should have a mammogram every year and should continue to do so for as long as they are in good health.* Clinical breast exam: *Women in their 20s and 30s should have a clinical breast exam (CBE) as part of a regular exam by a health expert preferably every 3 years.* Breast awareness and breast self-exam (BSE): *BSE is an option for women starting in their 20s.*

With regard to breast care, our Dr. Webster says, "The good news is we are doing a better job at diagnosing this disease earlier and therefore affording many women longer and healthier lives." She also concurs with most studies that recommend that women be taught how to do a 'self breast exam' by their doctor and that they actually perform one themselves on a monthly basis. Further she states, "The studies are clear; the combination of breast self exams, exams by a medical professional and mammography helps save lives!!! For those who lack health insurance there are often state funded programs that provide mammograms to low income women."

For women interested in ways of preventing breast cancer, check with your doctors regarding new studies involving aerobic exercise. On the NBC Today Show, March 20, 2007, Miriam Nelson, Associate Professor at the Friedman School of Nutrition at Tufts University stated that several new studies have shown that 4 to 5 hours a week of rigorous aerobic exercise may reduce one's risk of getting breast cancer an average of 31 percent.

And for some survivors of beast cancer, there is also very good news. It was reported on the Fox News segment, Fox RX,

> on April 27, 2005, by Dr. Steven Garner, current Chairman of Radiology at New York Methodist Hospital and former advisor to the city of New York in the wake of the 911 terrorist attacks, that a certain new drug, Herceptin, is effective at preventing breast cancer from reoccurring. Dr. Garner cautions that the medication is not good for all breast cancer survivors, but it could help approximately 62,000 women in America each year. The doctor recommends that breast cancer survivors, who are in remission visit their doctors for an evaluation to see if the treatment would be appropriate for them.
>
> For more detailed information regarding breast cancer, breast examinations and breast cancer prevention, we encourage you to visit the American Cancer Association's website at www.cancer.org.

Healthful Hints are for information only;
for medical advice see a doctor.

14. Don't Let Her Body Size Fool You. Men have had more discussions in bars, in nightclubs, on golf courses, on soccer fields, bowling alleys, basketball courts, and the like about the size of a woman's vagina based on her body size or type, or vis-à-vis a particular part of her body anatomy. Theories abound. Some are racial, ethnic, and cultural, you name it. I've even got a few theories of my own. The list is long and varied. I've heard that the women with the biggest vaginas are: the small women, or the skinny women, or the big breasted women, or the small breasted women, or the tall women, or the really huge Amazon women, or the big leg women, or the big hip women, or the big butt women, or the flat butt women, or the women whose nipples get hard, or the women that gave birth to more kids, and it goes on and on and on.

In almost every case, physiological or medical consideration has never found its way into the debate. It's just pure unadulterated male, "I know because I know" syndrome. And to that thinking I must admit that me, Roberto, I'm also guilty—because I think it's the skinny girls. Yet, what's even more fascinating is that lots of women are just as curious, but most won't admit it. Several women that I've dated have often asked me questions regarding the size, shape and other aspects of their vaginas as compared to that of other females. And I quite understand, cause how else would they know? So let's see how the experts sized it up.

All the experts seem to agree that the average adult woman's vagina is 3 to 4 inches long and extremely flexible. Although during intercourse the vagina stretches to accommodate a man's penis, that's not the full story. According to the book, *A Lifetime of Sex*, authors Stephen C. George and Ken Winston Caine note, "More remarkably, the vagina expands to far greater dimensions in order to become the birth canal during childbirth. (The biggest baby ever born was a 30-inch-long, 23-pound, 12-ounce behemoth to a Canadian woman in 1879, according to The Guinness Book of World Records.)"

Now, come on, let's be real. If a woman's vagina can handle 30 inches and 23 pounds, then I really don't think it matters what size the woman is nor the size of any of her body parts; she can certainly handle a man's little 6 inches, chew it up and spit it back out.

And though the experts did not make *any* correlation between the size of a woman's vagina and her body size or type, or with the size of any of her body parts, I'm sure the debate will rage on—so I still say it's the skinny girls. However, for some strange reason, women tend to feel that regardless of size, men think all vaginas are the same. Well, it may be true they all serve the same purpose, but, trust me, they are not all the same. Perhaps it's just that vaginas are like *Lite Beer* from Miller, some "taste great" and some are "less filling."

E. Healthful Hints: Obesity and Weight

While there may be no real medical correlation between the size of one's penis or vagina based on the size of any individual body parts, the overall size of the person can matter as it relates to good sexual health.

Licking the Myths

According to the American Obesity Association, "Obesity is a disease that affects nearly one-third of the adult American population (approximately 60 million). The number of overweight and obese Americans has continued to increase since 1960, a trend that is not slowing down. Today, 64.5 percent of adult Americans (about 127 million) are categorized as being overweight or obese. Each year, obesity causes at least 300,000 excess deaths in the United States, and healthcare costs of American adults with obesity amount to approximately $100 billion. Obesity is the second leading cause of unnecessary deaths. Obesity increases one's risk of developing conditions such as high blood pressure, diabetes (type 2), heart disease, stroke, gallbladder disease and cancer of the breast, prostate and colon."

Because being overweight can have such a profound affect on many other conditions that may affect ones general and sexual health, treatment should be sought for those suffering from obesity.

One very easy way to help with weight loss is just by increasing one's walking. An article, "Walk Off The Weight," by Selene Yeager, featured in the 2005 spring edition of Prevention Guide Magazine, stated, "In a recent study of 179 overweight men and women, researchers at the University of Pennsylvania found that those who boosted their walking by 5000 steps a day (a little over 2 miles) lost as much weight as those doing 50 minutes of structured aerobic activity four times a week."

To add, bodyandfitness.com says that burning fat cannot only be easy, it can also be fun. As they reported, "A 120-pound woman can burn over 4 extra calories per minute during sex. Ladies – It's too bad most men only last about five minutes (20 calories)."

For more detailed information regarding obesity, we encourage you to visit the American Obesity Association's website at www.obesity.org. Also, to find out how many calories you should consume and how much you should eat from each food category based on the United States government's current food pyramid, visit www.MyPyramid.gov.

Healthful Hints are for information only;
for medical advice see a doctor.

***15.* No Sex, Period!** Many couples wonder and argue whether or not it's okay to have sex while she's on her period. Well, it should be blood, sweat and no fears, because it's completely all right. Sari Locker, author of *The Complete Idiot's Guide To Amazing Sex*, says, "Sex during a woman's period might seem gross to some people.... It's really a matter of personal preference. A woman has just as much sexual sensation during her period, so if she and her partner want to have sex, they can."

Also in the book, *SEX: A Man's Guide* by Stefan Bechtel & Laurence Roy Stains, the authors write, "If you're certain she's not HIV positive and you don't mind a little additional mess, there's absolutely no reason not to make love while she's having her period." They further state, "Plenty of other people do. Of the thousands of men polled for the *Hite Report on Male Sexuality*, 67 percent said they enjoyed making love during her menses. And William H. Masters, M.D., and Virginia E. Johnson, of the former Masters and Johnson Institute in St. Louis, found that out of 331 women they studied, only 33 objected to having sex during menstruation (either for religious reasons or because of all that extra laundry)." *The Hite Report* also stated that 74% of the 436 women they surveyed reported an increase in sexual desire just before and during menstruation. So go ahead, you red-hot lovers—enjoy!

7. Healthful Hints: Vaginal Bleeding

According to emedicinehealth.com, "Unexpected bleeding is always a concern for any woman at any stage of life. Anything other than a normal menstrual period and even an abnormally heavy period can be great cause for alarm."

In an article asking the question, "What's considered irregular or abnormal vaginal bleeding? Andrew Good, M.D., an obstetrician and gynecologist at the Mayo Clinic, Rochester, Minnesota had this to say, "Irregular vaginal bleeding may include spotting of small amounts of blood between periods—often seen on toilet tissue after wiping—or heavy periods in which you soak a pad an hour for several hours. Any vaginal bleeding for weeks at a time also is considered irregular."

On whether one should be concerned or not, the doctor says, "It depends on your age and the circumstances. If you're premenopausal, light spotting a couple of days before your period is common and not worrisome. And if you're starting on birth control pills, you may experience occasional spotting the first few months. If you're menopausal or postmenopausal and are on hormone therapy on a cyclic regimen—taking oral estrogen daily plus oral progestin for 10 to 12 days a month—you may experience some bleeding resembling a period for a few days out of the month. This is known as withdrawal bleeding. If you have any vaginal bleeding other than the expected withdrawal bleeding, contact your doctor."

For more detailed information regarding vaginal bleeding, we encourage you to visit, www.MayoClinic.com

Healthful Hints are for information only; for medical advice see a doctor.

16. **Age Ain't Nothin' But A Number….** Many have thought that age was a death sentence that slowly crept up on those who wanted to keep having sex as they got older. Especially some men who may be approaching that time in their life when they begin worrying whether there's some truth to the statement, "Men are like bananas—the older they get the less firm they are." The truth is—when it comes to age and sex, age ain't nothin' but a number. Maturity provides an opportunity to make sex better and more satisfying than ever before.

According to *The Complete Idiot's Guide To Amazing Sex*, "People of any age can still experience total joy and pleasure from their sexuality. The sexual organs remain sexually sensitive for life and so can you." Furthermore, as stated in *The Hite Report*, 57 percent of men between the ages of 61 and 75 said their desire for sex either remained steady or increased with age. So, remember, loving never grows old.

Co-Host of NBC's *Today Show*, Ann Curry, reported on August 23, 2007 that, "The largest study ever about the sexual behavior of older Americans finds that you're never too old to get hot and heavy." Dr. Stacey Lindau of the University of Chicago headed the study, which was published in the New England Journal of Medicine and surveyed a cross section of more than 3000 people from age 57 to 85. Dr. Lindau stated, "Among men and women who have a sexual partner, the frequency of sexual activity is not very different than younger people who have a sexual partner. So we see in our study that men and women with a partner report in engaging in sexual activity about 2-3 times a week."

This idea of ageless sex is also in keeping with Alex Comfort, M. B., D.Sc., author of *The New Joy of Sex*, who says, "Neither men nor women lose either sexual needs or sexual function with age. In men, the only important changes over the first seven decades are that spontaneous erection occurs less often (accordingly they need more direct penile stimulation from the woman), ejaculation takes longer to happen (which is an advantage), coital frequency tends to fall, but given an attractive and receptive partner, decent general health and an absence of the belief that one ought to run out of steam, active sex lasts as long as life." According to a very youthful 75-year-old LaFrancine Tate, of Berkeley, California, "The advantage of getting older is that you learn how to slow down and enjoy the journey." Author and poet, Oliver Wendell Holmes said, "To be seventy years young is sometimes far more cheerful and hopeful than to be forty years old."

G. Healthful Hints: Colon Health

As we get older there are certain medical problems where risk of disease increases with age, and cancer of the colon is one of them. The American Cancer Association notes that the exact cause of most colorectal cancer is not known, yet there are certain known risk factors of which one should be aware: 1) Having a family history of colorectal cancer; 2) Ethnic background: Jews of Eastern European descent, especially Ashkenazi Jews, have a higher rate of colon cancer; 3) Having had colorectal cancer previously; 4) Having a history of polyps; 5) Having a history of bowel disease; 6) Age: More than 9 out of 10 people found to have colorectal cancer are older than 50; 7) Diet: A diet high in fat, especially fat from animal sources, can increase the risk of colorectal cancer; 8) Lack of exercise and being overweight; 9) Smoking; 10) Heavy alcohol use.

Dr. Webster says, "Fortunately, we have good screening tests for colon cancer. Beginning at age 50 your doctor may recommend any of the following: fecal occult blood testing which requires that you, the patient, bring samples of stool to be tested for microscopic blood; flexible sigmoidoscopy, where a medical professional inserts a flexible, hollow tube into the rectum to visualize the surfaces of the lower portions of the colon; or colonoscopy, which allows a medical professional to visualize the entire colon to look at the internal surfaces of the intestines to make sure there are no tumors, polyps or other abnormalities. Although the procedure may be a bit uncomfortable, it is tolerable and has proven to aid in the diagnosis of very early stages of cancers. This, in turn, allows for increased survival and quality of life." Dr. Webster also agrees with the American Cancer Society, which strongly recommends obtaining a colonoscopy-screening exam for colon cancer, even if you are feeling well without any symptoms at all, at age 50. Dr. Webster says it does save lives!

The ACS Guidelines suggest, beginning at age 50, both men and women at average risk should be screened and those who are at above average risk should be screened earlier. As Dr. Webster mentioned, there are several tests used to screen for colorectal cancer and different options for those with an average risk of colorectal cancer. Ask your doctor which tests are available where you live and which option is best for you.

> For more detailed information regarding colon cancer and its consequences, we encourage you to visit the American Cancer Association's website at www.cancer.org.

*Healthful Hints are for information only;
for medical advice see a doctor.*

17. Douche, Douche In the Bush? Many women feel the need and believe it necessary to unnaturally clean and sweeten the smell of their vagina by using feminine perfumes and deodorants. However, the experts say not so. Sari Locker in *The Complete Idiot's Guide To Amazing Sex*, says, "The vagina is a self cleaning organ. Just showering washes away any normal vaginal discharge and odor. So-called 'female deodorants' or douching of any kind is unnecessary and, in fact, can be harmful. Perfumes or chemicals included in these products may irritate the vaginal tissues and could even lead to vaginal infections. Do not use these! Shower to remove the natural odor. Do not try to add a floral smell to your crotch. Although they may look like flowers, vaginas should not smell like them."

Further emphasizing the point, in *The New Joy of Sex*, author Alex Comfort, M. B., D.Sc., says, "Indiscriminate douching is medically a bad idea in any case—the vagina is self-cleaning and water merely upsets its natural hygiene. Keep the douche, and the bidet, for cleaning up after menstrual periods." And another doctor stated, "Don't use vinegar and water to douche, remember your vagina is not a pickle; so it's no need to pickle your puss."

It is completely normal for women to have a clear mucous or a whitish discharge. However, if you are experiencing an unusual discharge that has a disagreeable odor, texture, or color, it may be due to infection and should be examined by your medical doctor for proper treatment.

18. PMS: Is It Is or Is It Ain't? As crazy and grammatically incorrect as the question was posed, is just about how crazy and incorrect some men think women behave when they claim they are "PMS-ing."

Many men believe there's no such thing, and that women are always PMS-ing: Pre, Post and Present! Though the acronym is supposed to represent, Premenstrual Syndrome, some men think it's just an excuse women use for behaving badly. However, some women say it's just, "Putting-up with Men's Shit." Many women, who don't suffer from PMS often don't believe the women who say they do. Nevertheless, for you doubting Thomases and Thomasines, I'm sorry to report that the medical experts all agree, Premenstrual Syndrome does exist.

PMS occurs as a result of numerous hormonal changes that take place in a woman's body prior to her menstrual cycle, which may cause her to experience a multitude of symptoms. These may include: headaches, backaches, body aches, depression, mood swings, stress, cramps, irritability, bloating, breast tenderness, unusual urges, cravings for sweets, and just a general bad attitude. So you guys, friends, relatives and lovers all might as well sit back, relax and just get use to it, because the doctors suggest, *there's no cure for this*!

19. **Masturbation Will Make You Go Blind...** As the old adage goes, "If masturbation will make me go blind, can I do it till I just need glasses?" My friends and I use to laugh about those lines, but I never quite understood why we put so much onus on anything that involves our sexual organs. It's as if they were somehow different than an arm or leg—I thought they were all just parts of our body. It has always been puzzling to me that if you touched or massaged your arm or leg and it felt good, that's okay; however, if you touched or massaged your penis or vagina and it felt good, you've done a terrible thing and should be castigated and go to hell for it.

Most medical professionals and sex therapists agree that masturbation is safe and natural; however, because of various religious ideas and attitudes towards it, many still think of masturbation as a sinful act; thus, causing it to remain shrouded in mystery, guilt and shame; something you dare not talk about openly.

In recent times, it seems the veil of shame has been somewhat lifted, but not quite all the way. Many single people and married couples alike, even though they masturbate regularly, still feel some sense of guilt. It has been reported that as many as 90% of men and more than 80% of women have masturbated—so stop feeling bad about it, we all can't be wrong.

According to *The Complete Idiot's Guide To Amazing Sex*, author Sari Locker says, "…You have to get rid of those nagging feelings that tell you that masturbation is something you need to feel guilty about. I'm telling you once and for all that touching yourself is the most natural thing in the world. Masturbation is for all of us: young, old, married, single, happy, or sad. Masturbation is sex with someone you love. Feel pride in self-pleasure. Don't be afraid to mention the word anymore. There is no need to feel ashamed!" As a matter of fact, self-pleasuring has a very storied past. In ancient Greece during the Pederastic period when men found it fashionable to be sexually involved with young boys, many women resorted to using dildos, which they oddly enough called pacifiers. And more than a thousand years prior, in an ancient Egyptian myth, the creator God Atum was said to have created the origins of the universe and all of mankind by stimulating himself through masturbation.

For those of you, who may not know exactly what it means to masturbate, a simple definition would be, To give oneself or somebody else sexual pleasure by stroking the genitals or other body parts, including the breasts, chest, thighs, lips, buttocks, and anus, usually to orgasm. In many circles, masturbation is sometimes referred to as: self-stimulation, autoeroticism, self-pleasuring and by many other clever names. Yet we all know that a rose by any other name still smells just as sweet; and masturbation by any other name still feels just as good. Here are a few of the more common names that might give you a rise:

Beating Your Meat	*Jilling Off*
Bleeding the Weasel	*Hacking the Hog*
Bopping the Baloney	*Playing with Yourself*
Burping the Worm	*Pocket Pool*
Choking the Chicken	*Roping the Pony*
Cleaning Your Rifle	*Slamming the Hammer*
Five-Finger Shuffle	*Shooting Your Load*

Licking the Myths

Flogging the Dog *Spanking the Monkey*
Flying Solo *Taming the One Eyed Monster*
Getting Yourself Off *Walking the Dog*
Jacking Off *Whacking Off*
Jerking Off *Whipping the Willie*

As funny and whacky as some of the names are, there is more to masturbation than meets the eye, the hand, or the vibrator. There are great benefits to autoeroticism. First and foremost, it helps you to discover what it takes for you to respond sexually. This will help you more clearly communicate what really pleases you to your partner. With practice, it may help men learn to control their ejaculatory responses, leading to more pleasurable sexual experiences. Further, for some women who find it difficult to have an orgasm, and for many women who have never had an orgasm, masturbation may actually teach them how. Also, self-pleasuring may relieve stress for some, act as a natural sleeping aid and help you with bouts of sexual frustration as well. In addition, it can provide single people with a sexual alternative other than "one night stands" and dates with undesirable mates "just for the sex of it." Masturbation is the ultimate way to practice safe sex and birth control. Furthermore, it can literally keep you "wet" during your sexual dry spells. For men and women alike, it won't change the shape or size of your genitals.

Tantric Secrets, 7 Steps To The Best Sex Of Your Life, weighs in on the matter by saying, "In order to connect with your sexual energy, make love to yourself." It also recommends how men and women should best go about it. It recommends, "Women: Oil your genitals all over—your inner thighs, vulva, inner lips and your anus. Explore the delicate skin on the inside of your thighs, perhaps stroking your breasts at the same time. Touch your inner and outer lips, and all the surfaces of your genitals. Play around the clitoris, using a finger on each side to rub up and down. Circle around the clitoris, or gently rub the hood over the clitoris. Take plenty of time in order to find out what feels delicious, and to immerse yourself in your own pleasure.

Men: Try different strokes and ways of touching yourself. Use your hand to hold your penis with your thumb facing up or down. Use one hand or two to cradle your genitals. Use your hand to make a ring around your penis. Roll your penis between your hands, or use rhythmic, stroking movements up and down its length. Cradle your scrotum, and rub or gently squeeze. Rub the fleshy mound behind your scrotum, which is the external prostate spot. As you get aroused by stroking your genitals, you may like to explore the perineum (the area between the scrotum and anus) and the anus, as this area becomes more pleasurable when engorged with blood."

An added erotic bonus of masturbation for some may be to allow your partner to watch you or take turns getting each other off. There are a variety of methods and styles of masturbation: fantasies, sex toys, vibrators, pictures, magazines, X-rated flicks, dirty talk, phone sex, chat lines and so on. Try experimenting with masturbation together and enjoy discovering the many different ways of pleasuring yourself and each other.

If you are in a married or committed relationship and your partner still masturbates, it doesn't mean that you do not turn them on. To quote Sari Locker again, "It may just mean that they still like getting turned on by themselves, or that they have a higher sex drive than their partner and they just need a little something to supplement their sex life…" However, Sari does go on to say, "In a good relationship, sex with your partner should take precedence over masturbation…" So, no matter how much you enjoy pleasuring yourself, it should not replace having sex with your partner. If that starts to happen you should talk about it and possibly seek the help of a sex therapist as it could lead to problems in your relationship.

Now that you're sure you won't go blind if you masturbate too much, you still may be in danger of developing Carpal Tunnel Syndrome.

20. Hell Hath No Fury Like A Woman Scorned? Lorena Bobbitt chopped off her husband's penis, Andree Rene set her boyfriend's penis on fire, Clara Harris ran over her husband three times in a Mercedes Benz, Juanita Jones shot rhythm and blues superstar Jackie Wilson, Mary Woodson poured boiling hot grits on blues singer Al Green and Frankie shot Johnny. Thus, one would have to assume that the myth of the scorned woman may be true. There could possibly be only a few other creatures that may exhibit more fury than a woman: King Kong, Godzilla, or maybe the Incredible Hulk, but I wouldn't bet on it. So men, you need to be extremely careful regarding the comments you make to women, the manner in which you express things to them, the things you may do to hurt them, your overall treatment of them, and most importantly, you don't want to be found guilty of indulging in any illicit affairs!

Women are such passionate and emotional beings, and it's absolutely wonderful when they use their passion and emotion in a loving way. But they can be like "hell-fire" when forced to exhibit that same passion and emotion scornfully. Moreover, they have memories like elephants; especially about some event that affected them emotionally.

Women have the ability to vividly remember things that men have long forgotten, and they almost always seem to recall it at the most inopportune time. It could be days, weeks, or even years later. Just imagine yourself lying in bed with the aroma of fresh jasmine and the sound of soft music oozing into the atmosphere as the twinkle from the candlelight is being reflected off of the Waterford crystal wine glasses. Then here she comes looking oh so gorgeous in a sexy black negligee—sliding her head in between your legs making you hot as a firecracker.

Next, she starts talking sexy to you, and you answer, "Yeah baby go ahead, do it!" You watch as she slowly makes that move to go down on you. Then she looks you in the eye and grabs your rock hard penis as she takes her soft silky tongue and licks it surrounding the tip with her sweet juicy lips—when BAM it hits her! She lifts her head up and sneers at you with that scornful look of vengeance, "Yeah that's right," she says. "I remember it now."

As you quip, "Baby, remember what? What are you talking about? Come on, don't stop now—can't we talk about this later?"

"No we can't," she says angrily, while clutching her hand tighter at the base of your penis. "That's what you told me the last time, so I think we should talk about it right now, while I have your full undivided attention!" That's when your rock hard penis immediately turns to Jell-O.

She furiously continues with that scorned woman look, "It was six years ago in June. It was partly cloudy. I remember like it was yesterday—you had on that beautiful blue shirt that I bought you for your birthday and some nice gray slacks when I caught you with that Bitch! Then, as if you thought I was born yesterday, you had the nerve to tell me she was your cousin." Need I continue? I think we all know how that story ended. His funeral was later that week....

So guys, I hope you know what you are doing; and if you don't, let this be a warning.

You *must* be very mindful of what you say and do to her. Women are *blessed*—and they are by far one of God's most favored creatures, endowed with special powers you can't even imagine. She can hear through walls—like a wiretap she can provide a word-for-word transcript of the conversation you thought you were sneaking and had gotten away with. She has X-ray vision—and can spot a lipstick stain on your shirt from across 3 rooms, even after you lied and said it was just taco sauce and tried to remove it with cold water and club soda. She has a hound dog's sense of smell—and can detect another woman's perfume after you've intentionally poured liquor on your shirt and drove all the way home with the windows down in the dead of winter trying to disguise it. Her intuition is like a lie detector—and can have you confessing things you hadn't even thought about doing.

So if you think you're Superman and she's just some weak damsel in distress, well, you better think again. Yes, she may be physically weaker than you, but she also has a storehouse full of Kryptonite; and when her fury comes, you know not the day nor the hour. So before you allow her to put your penis in her mouth, (as they say on the street), "you better recognize," and get rid of all the skeletons in your closet—because, hell hath no fury like a woman scorned… and trust me, *that's* no myth!

Haunted Dreams

why do u come to
HAUNT ME in MY DREAMS?
after 2 cans of DRANO, LIQUID PLUMBER
and several strokes of the PLUNGER,
i thought i had FLUSHED u out of my system—
but somehow u still manage to
HAUNT ME in MY DREAMS.
but now i've got me a new plumber,
*and i've had some **new** PIPE INSTALLED,*
and it FITS GOOD! and maybe that will keep u
from clogging up my system,
obstructing my flow & invading my dreams.
i need
***no**—**re**-evaluating,*
***no** painful—**re**-minders,*
***no** mirrored—**re**-flections,*
***no** clever—**re**-telling,*
***no** dramatic—**re**-creations,*
***no** instant—**re**-plays,*
***no** critical—**re**-views,*
***no** scenes—**re**-calling,*
ME & U...
no photo-static copies of my heart,
that i signed over to u on a blank check
*to put in YOUR **SAFE** DEPOSIT BOX,*
that U instead cashed & invested
in somebody else's LOVE ACCOUNT.

*so i-don't-want-U-in-**MY**-DREAMS!*
re-minding me in Panavision, Technicolor, 3D, 4D, HD, Imax,
Special EFX, Surround Sound, Dolby and THX
that U disappeared, fled, checked out, left, went,
split, disembarked & abandoned ship—
using MY HEART as YOUR LIFE RAFT
while leaving me to drown ALL-BY-MYSELF…
so u need to keep yo' lyin, cheatin', selfish, ungrateful,
always apologizin', sorry ass out-of-MY-DREAMS—
***THEY** belong to **ME**! you've already taken my heart,*
so HONEY PLEEEEASE—
at least let me have MY DREAMS…
but Baby u know, it's just like u to-show-up-IN-A-DREAM—
'cause u were NEVER-EVER MUCH
ON BEING FOR REAL!!!

Julie Lovelace

Licking the Myths

"Ssss ooh, I just love the way you make me feel..."

"Before making love—don't hesitate to communicate…"

Chapter Three

Things to Say or Do Before Sex

*I*f you follow these simple and easy steps, we're certain your love life will be much better for it. Most of the information contained herein you may already be familiar with, but have just failed to put into practice. So, for some of you, it may be a matter of just refreshing your memory; for others it may be invaluable new knowledge. But for everyone, it remains the key to making your relationship much better; and having a wonderful relationship is what leads to a much better sex life and a more pleasurable love life.

While You Are There

*It's not Always how Early you come…
Nor is it Always how Late you stay…but sometimes,
It's just what you do While You Are There.*

Julie Lovelace

21. Know Thy Self and Love Thy Self.... It's a good idea to analyze oneself. We tend to know a great deal more about the needs, wants and desires of others than we do about ourselves. Perhaps Lao Tse said it best— "He who knows others is clever; he who knows himself is enlightened." So make it a point to get to know "you," your strengths as well as your weaknesses. Scrutinize yourself with the same curiosity and zeal as you do potential lovers. You may be surprised at what you'll find.

Try to make an honest assessment of the things you do well and weigh seriously the other aspects you'd like to improve. If that proves too difficult for you to manage alone, ask friends and loved ones to help you with it. Once you truly know yourself—your real likes and dislikes, your true needs and desires, your strengths and weaknesses—you'll be able to better communicate these qualities to your lover. According to the *Kundalini Research Institute International Training Manual Level 1*, "It is essential to be clear about your our own needs. Do not wait for the other person to know what to do. Try asking, 'What do I need?' When we ourselves know what we need, it is easier to communicate it. When we do not know what we need or how to communicate it, how can the other person know our need?"

When sharing with your lover all that you've discovered about yourself and what you need, it's okay to be aggressive and confident, but not pushy and cocky; you can be strong and determined, but not forceful and overbearing. And be careful to never promise more than you can deliver. If you need to make any declarations about what you can do, understate it and let your lover be pleasantly surprised by your performance. It's better to under promise and over deliver. Don't boast repeatedly about how great you are at *this* or how fantastic you are at *that* when you're just getting to know someone; unless of course, that's just the kind of person you really are. However, very few people prefer to be with someone who is conceited and brags about himself all the time—unless of course, that person is Muhammad Ali.

After getting to know yourself, you must learn to love yourself. As it says in *Tantric Secrets, 7 Steps To The Best Sex Of Your Life,*

"…the secret of maintaining a loving relationship is to love yourself. You learn to love yourself by taking care of your needs; when you nurture yourself, you have the resources to nurture others."

It's worth emphasizing that after you've become intimately acquainted with yourself, it's okay to love yourself; but be sure not to fall *in* love with yourself. Narcissism often leads to selfishness, and selfishness has no place in loving relationships. There may be different strokes for different folks, but I know of no one who likes a selfish lover. So be very mindful of selfish behavior; it may cause others to withhold greater things from you than you're protecting and holding for yourself. The ultimate goal in a true loving relationship is for each partner to become "selfless" and *one* with the other.

22. In Love We Trust… When it "comes" to having great sex or great lovemaking, trust is the most important ingredient—period! The end! Without it, you might as well forget about ever achieving your full potential for ecstasy when having sex and making love. Yet, trust is viewed differently between men and women.

What weighs most on a man's ability to be trusted is his desire to have "new sex," or as comedian Chris Rock refers to it, "new pussy." Most men have a true fascination with new or different sex. While both men and women may talk about fantasy sexual encounters, men are more likely to try to make their fantasy come true. Most often, what affects a man's ability to be trusted is that he can more easily have non-emotional, "loveless" sex. This ability to have sex without love enables men to have multiple sex partners without any thought of an emotional consequence; thereby making it much more difficult for them to be trusted.

On the other hand, because most women prefer, desire, and in some instances even require an emotional element (or some feelings of love) when having sex, it makes it much more unlikely that they'll have as many sex partners as men; thus, making it much easier to trust them. Like most things in life, it's a numbers game.

Often with men, just new sex alone is reason enough to make them want to do it, even though this may be risking a loving relationship and even a great marriage. Numerous times when men are caught cheating and their mates ask, "Why did you sleep with *her*, seeing that she wasn't that attractive and didn't have very much to offer?" The frequent answer, "I don't know," which, translated, means it was just new sex. Conversely, if the new sex partner is gorgeous, the answer is, "The devil made me do it, so don't be mad at me; just pray for me." But men, take note. A Chinese proverb says, "It take many nails to build house of love, but only one wrong *screw* to bring it down."

So men, because your reputation for trust and fidelity isn't that sparkling and you truly value your relationship, when she confronts you with some probing trust related questions, if you really have nothing to hide, don't hide anything—just answer the questions and reassure her rather than getting angry and defensive about it. Once a pattern of honesty and trust is established, those probing questions should go away.

You see, everything sexually, and the relationship itself, begins and ends with trust; and that's especially true for women. The *Kundalini Research Institute International Teacher Training Manual Level 1*, affirms that, "A woman has to trust and feel that the relationship is secure in order to thoroughly relax." So guys, don't try to trick your lover into doing something by lying about it or deceiving her. If you invest the time and effort to gain her confidence and trust, she will do almost anything to please you.

As a F.Y.I for you men, during our research for this book, the single most requested trait that women wanted in their men was honesty. So upon meeting women for the first time be honest and sincere; she will appreciate that much more than she would some phony sounding "pick-up" lines. Please guys, no mention of your astrological sign, and don't tell her that she looks like someone you use to know. Don't flash any jewelry, talk about what kind of car you drive or the material things you may possess. As educator Tamara Moore instructs, "Never allow material things to *define* you, but rather use them to complement you." Make no insincere remarks about how she looks or what she's wearing. Women know much more than they reveal, so don't placate! Moreover, don't mention your profession unless she asks you, or, unless it comes about as a natural part of the conversation. Don't brag about yourself, but rather let her *discover* some of the wonderful things about you. Lastly, don't try to *sell* yourself to her; instead, let your personality and *who* you are sell you.

On the other hand, ladies, if you want your man to trust you, you should never mislead him to believe you're offering him a choice when you're really not. Men hate it when you give them a choice of "this" or "that," then get upset when he chooses "that." If there is something in particular you want him to do or a choice you want him to make, then just say so. Learn to make clear, concise and direct requests as to what you truly desire. As a rule, just be honest, forthright and sincere.

It is of the utmost importance that you realize that trust and honesty dictate that you make your lover aware if you have any drug, alcohol, gambling, shopping or any other dependency problems (including cigarettes and food) early on in your relationship. And for those of you who have suffered any past experiences with sexual trauma or domestic violence (and you feel comfortable enough), then certainly let your partner know, so that they may be sensitive to those concerns. And if you're in a committed relationship, marriage or with someone that you truly care about, you may want them to understand these issues and maybe even ask them to attend counseling with you.

We should add jealously to the list, which in many ways is a dependency and lack of trust issue. If you know that you have a tendency toward being jealous, it may serve you well to inform your lover from the onset. This honest acknowledgment may allow them to include behaviors to reassure you, before the jealousy starts to cause problems in your relationship. In today's world, people are much more understanding of these issues and if discussed openly and honestly, up-front, it may add to the potential success of the relationship.

Love is, finally, about trust; and if love is about trust, then great sex and lovemaking have to include trust, too. So if you truly want to be loved, make it an important part of your life to be trustworthy and worthy of your lover's trust.

23. **Looks Can Be Deceiving**, because what you see is *not* always what you get—when it comes to love, you frequently get much less than what you see. So don't overestimate one's sexual potential or his or her ability or capability to be a "loving person" based on looks.

We've all been told, "One should never judge a book by its cover," yet, most everyone does. However, even though looks *can* be deceiving, sometimes they're not that far off. We've all heard the phrase, "If it looks like a duck, walks like a duck and quacks like a duck, it's a duck!" Or at least it may be a quail, a pheasant, a seagull, but certainly not a lion! I'm somewhat playing both sides, because either side is often true. The lesson for you is to not make *your* looks deceiving, because most people looking *at* you do believe that "looks are everything," and that "what you see *is* what you get." Learn to look, act and be who you are.

Meanwhile, looks do count. So make it a habit to look your best at all times. But don't misunderstand what I'm saying; it's *your* looks that count, not how you look compared to others. Always keep up *your* personal appearance and don't worry about how you look compared to your "so called" competition. He or she may seem more physically attractive than you; however, there are two things you must know: "beauty is in the eye of the beholder," and "beauty is only skin deep." Also keep in mind that cultural preferences play an important role in physical attraction. What may be considered a very attractive feature in one culture, may hold little sex appeal in another. Strong support for this idea can be found in *The Big Black Book*, under the heading of, *What Men Love In Women*: "The trait men first associate with a beautiful woman: 42% say personality, 23% think of the smile, 13% say eyes, and only 6% zero in on the body." So, in the end, it's *who* you are and your behavior that really counts most. Remember, if your lover is *that* hung-up on looks, the relationship won't last anyway, because then he or she will always be in search of someone who looks better.

People rarely end up with what they perceive to be their fantasy mates. Take celebrities for example and look at their mates. They could probably have whomever they want. Yet, the prettiest girls are not always found with the most handsome guys and vice versa. That's because, although a great looker can catch your attention, looks alone will rarely keep it. When it comes to love, you'll be surprised to know that what you may think to be the most logical answer is not always true. A survey by *The Big Black Book* defies what most of us would take to be obvious, it stated, "Those who have the toughest time finding acceptable dates: (1) Very beautiful women. Men are afraid to approach them. When they do, it's usually not for the right reasons. (2) Very successful men. Women stay away from them because they feel such men have so many other choices, creating too much competition." So unless you are a *very* beautiful women or *very* successful man, you have a much better chance than you think you do of finding that special someone.

The real lesson here is how *you* look and how you use the way *you* look. So just look *your* best and don't worry about the rest. If looks were *so* damn important, why is it that when most people get ready to make love the first thing they do is turn off the lights? It's truly how one looks *inside* that really counts.

Remember these few things. The smile is universally recognized and understood by all cultures. According to the *Discovery Science Channel*, on its popular TV series *Megascience*, in an episode discussing searching for the secrets of sex appeal, they had this to say regarding the smile. "It is known to be the most appealing expression of all in human body language." So don't be afraid to smile more often.

And have you ever wondered why bright red lipstick is the world's most popular color? Well again, *Megascience* reported that, "Sociologists say that glossy red lips mimic the female sex organs." They further note that professional image consultants exclaim that black and red are the most powerful colors, and that red is the first color a man sees. And when it comes to the sexiest aromas, they stressed that natural vanilla and night blooming jasmine were considered the most sensual.

Special tips for you ladies. Only wear as much makeup as you actually need. Don't overdo it. According to a survey in *The Complete Idiot's Guide To Amazing Sex*, "Almost 75 percent (of men) agreed that the thing that they found the most unattractive was when a woman wears heavy makeup." High on another list of turn-offs were excessive weight and arrogance.

Looks Can Be Deceiving

most times, the new **Loves** we discover
meet **Our Eyes** before they meet **Our Hearts**...
and before we venture to take our new found
Love
on that arduous trip to visit **Our Hearts,**
we usually come upon a fork in the road...
and often times
the journey to **Our Hearts**
becomes the road not taken...
as **Our Eyes** lead us to travel the road
that looks paved and smooth—tree lined and picturesque—
which **is** most pleasing to **Our Eyes**...
even though the road sign above clearly reads,
"Dead End Ahead."
you see, **Our Eyes** are very selfish,
and would much rather travel a smooth looking road
that leads to **Nowhere**—
than traverse the unsightly cobblestone path with the steep hill
that leads to **Paradise**...
we must learn the search for true
Love
is much too important a task to be relegated to **Our Eyes** alone—
the Mind, Body, Soul and Spirit **must** participate...
because,
Looks Can Be Deceiving

R. Ray Barnes

24. **Foreplay Is All Day, 24/7.** So, make it a habit to always behave in a loving way towards your partner. From the moment you're awake, foreplay should begin. It could be a sexy smile, a playful pat on the butt, a light kiss somewhere, a sexy note placed to be easily discovered, a hug and a whisper of a promise you're going to fulfill later, a "talking nasty" phone call in the middle of the day, a sexy voicemail message or a little sexting. Don't merely restrict your foreplay to the bedroom at night. Playfully flirt with your lover everywhere. Touch, tease, kiss and squeeze something on your lover throughout the day. Just get in the habit of saying and doing something sensuous to your lover at unexpected times.

Try doing some of the things you used to when you were a teenager, before you were actually ready to have sex. You know, the way you'd grind to a slow song and those things you did that caused the windows to steam at the drive-in movies. Re-live the way you use to cuddle, rub and caress each other that made you both so hot. Learn how to tempt, persuade and romantically attract your lover. Be seductive!

Sharing a nice hot fragrant bubble bath by candlelight is a wonderful way to start an evening of erotic lovemaking and romance. Water can be very comfortable, relaxing and sensual. Showers can be sensuous too. And in most cases, take your time. Foreplay is often best in slow motion.

Men especially, you mustn't take foreplay lightly. According to a survey conducted by researchers at Lu Wan Maternity and Child Health Hospital, Peoples Republic of China, published in the *Journal of Psychology and Human Sexuality*, almost twice the percentage of married women were dissatisfied with their sex lives versus that of their husbands. The main factors that influenced a wife's sexual satisfaction were the amount of foreplay and when and if she had an orgasm....

25. **Guys, Ladies Love to Receive Flowers** and/or thoughtful gifts, especially when it's for no special occasion. Most women love to know that they're being thought of—it's a true aphrodisiac. Ladies, though men appreciate thoughtful gifts too, they'd rather receive it in the form of admiration from you. You see, underneath all of their macho "bulls#*%," men know they are the weaker sex; they just don't feel they can afford to admit it. It's similar to when the actor and sex symbol Rock Hudson admitted he was gay, it seemed to destroy the image some men believe they need to have of themselves. But when pressed hard enough, quietly and in private, some men may acknowledge that surrounding most great men is a great woman pushing and pulling them along while at the same time pointing the way—using their love like guard rails, they keep them on the path to glory. According to Yogi Bhajan, in the *Kundalini Research Institute International Teacher Training Manual Level 1*, "A man knows that he is limited, and he feels attracted to a woman who can give him what he is missing, or help him to develop different aspects of himself. He feels attracted to a woman because she can take him to a different level and experience. When a man really loves his wife, he will want her to develop herself and express her infinity, because then she can inspire him to realms beyond his own dreams."

I'm...Yours

I'm
Incurably Yours
& ***Lovingly*** Yours
& ***Affectionately*** Yours
& ***Passionately*** Yours
& ***Erotically*** Yours
—but mostly...
I'm ***Missing*** Yours

Bianca Baker/ R. Ray Barnes

So if you want a man to perform at his best, find something that he's done that you can legitimately tell him you're very proud of. The fact that you admire him and continuously feed his ego with good wholesome "ego treats" has the same affect as rubbing a puppy on his belly; he won't go anywhere until you stop. And most times thereafter, when he sees you he will automatically turn over on his back expecting you to rub his belly again.

Furthermore ladies, when you want to reward your man, reward him with something *he* likes and not with something *you* like. A cool reward for most men would probably not be a passionate hug and a kiss in the middle of a crowded shopping mall or a place where other men might see them. Just remember how your teenage son began to act when you wanted to kiss him in front of his friends. Well, sometimes men behave just like adult teenagers. They often respond like trained animals. So, if you'd like them to do something, simply give them a reward or a treat for each task they complete. Ego food is always their treat of choice; just make sure it's based on something factual or real—don't placate or fabricate. It's really too bad that men don't realize that *being cool* won't keep their love warm...

"Celebrate your love every chance you get..."

26. **Ladies, Your Hands and Feet Can Be Such A Sexy Turn-On** to men, but with your feet, some may even develop a fetish. Men with foot fetishes are quite common. Some men feel the need to touch, stroke, lick, suck or kiss a foot to attain orgasm. It may surprise you to know that many men talk about the appearance of a woman's feet to their friends.

Men think open toe shoes are sexy. So, if a woman has attractive, well-groomed feet and hands, I guarantee you men will take notice. Conversely, if she doesn't, men will note that even more! It's a definite plus if a woman has pretty feet and hands. With that in mind, it may do you well to maintain a fresh manicure and pedicure. If you are unable to do so, at least keep your nails clean and remove all chipped and cracked polish before meeting with or going out with a gentleman. And moderation may be best when it comes to acrylic nails, designs, and jewels.

Blanket Of Love

*Sometimes I don't take the time
to tell you that I truly appreciate
The Man that you are.
For being there when I need you,
For having a shoulder to lean on and tears to share.
I'm so thankful you **always** come when I call.
It feels so good to know that **You really** care...
It's your Blanket Of Love that keeps my heart warm.*

Bianca Baker/R. Ray Barnes

---

27. **Guys, Compliment the Ladies** when taking them out on a nice date. They spend hours preparing themselves to look beautiful just for you; let them know you've noticed. However, be specific rather than just saying, "You look nice." Feel free to add comments about what she's wearing, her hair, makeup, shoes, jewelry, etc. Women are very sensitive and it means a great deal for them to know that you actually pay attention to some of the small things. You see, everyone notices the pink elephant standing in the middle of the room, but few would spot the beautiful butterfly perched upon the crystal vase in the corner.

If you're planning to bring her back to your place, make sure your kitchen and bathrooms are clean; trust me, they will not only ask to use the bathroom, they will examine it as if it's a crime scene investigation. Leave no prescription medications exposed that you may not want them to see. I'm not saying they're nosy; however, women have been known at times to be quite curious; not generally so for men.

For some women, bathrooms are tantamount to sacred places; and as for a man's bathroom, cleanliness is next to Godliness. They'll never tell you, but many follow-up dates are lost because of a man's unclean bathroom. Women feel a clean bathroom says a lot about a man's personal hygiene; they're right, it does!

28. **Learn To Be A Good Kisser** and understand what kissing means to your partner. Kissing is very important and is usually the first sign of true intimacy. For most people, kissing may serve as a prelude to sex, but not always, so one must be careful to read your partners kiss properly. I know it may seem strange, but some consider kissing equal to or even more intimate than sexual intercourse. Most prostitutes who have protected sex will not kiss their Johns. So you don't want to "ass-u-me" the wrong thing from a kiss and move too quickly and get embarrassed.

There are many levels of kissing. Know what level you're on before you decide to jump out of the kissing window onto your butt. To get a true sense of the meaning of the kiss, read your partners body language and listen closely to what it's telling you, verbally and silently.

Usually passionate, wet-lip and deep tongue kisses at the right place and time can lead to a sexual encounter, but not always, so don't take anything for granted. However, in most cases, during sexual intercourse, wet-lip and deep tongue kisses can add greatly to the pleasure.

Her Kiss

It all started with
Her Kiss...
Followed by days of heavenly Bliss,
Didn't know such a feeling could Exist,
Until I tasted the sweetness of
Her Kiss...
Into the night our bodies did Twist,
Sinking deeper into ecstasy's Abyss,
As we both were caught in the Gist,
The fear of love hung in the Mist—
As I inhaled the sweetness of
Her Kiss...
If not for her my heart would be Remiss,
So wonderful and lovely was This,
Loving her made the top of my List,
Taste better than chocolate made by the Swiss—
I truly miss the sweetness of
Her Kiss...
Now I'm lying here trying to Resist,
As I close my eyes and Reminisce,
The cold sweats and hot dreams Persist,
So close to love but I wouldn't dare Insist—
Just captivated by the sweetness of
Her Kiss...
She is such a beautiful and intelligent Sis,
But she chose to Cease & Desist,
I'm so disappointed in love Boo Hiss,
I often wish that we could Re-enlist,
For a few more moments of heavenly Bliss—
That only "comes" from the sweetness of
Her Kiss...

R. Ray Barnes

Be aware that there are many different ways to kiss someone, and that kisses can be administered all over the body. Try making it a habit to use a variety of kisses. You can gently kiss the breast, neck, genitals, earlobes, eyelids, navel, hands, feet, fingers, toes—everywhere! You can also kiss someone on the buttocks or you can "kiss ass." However, you may not want to develop a reputation as a great ass kisser, but then again, to each his own. Kisses can be with ice, chocolate or whatever you like. Kissing has a way of bringing people closer together. So be creative and don't be afraid to make kissing an exciting adventure for you and your partner.

Whenever you plan to kiss someone, have fresh breath and avoid chapped lips if possible. If you happen to make a move to kiss someone before he or she is ready and willing, or if you encounter any resistance, try converting the kiss to a hug instead. Almost everyone likes being hugged.

29. **Guys, She Doesn't *Owe* You Anything** simply because you've taken her out on a nice date—dinner, movie, the theater, etc., so don't act like she does. If you want a prostitute, then get one. Don't expect a lady to act like one... unless she *wants* to.

30. **Honesty Is the Best Policy, So Ladies Don't Lead Him On.** If you know after a few expensive dates, that you have no genuine intentions of any relationship with the man, be woman enough to let him know. Then, if he chooses to keep spending his hard earned cash to take you out on expensive dates, he will know for sure not to expect anything in return.

Likewise guys, *honesty is the best policy* for you too. *Don't lead her on.* If you know that all you want from her is a sexual relationship or if you're married or serious about someone else, then be man enough to tell her the truth. Don't lie or mislead her about your real intentions. Give her the choice to decide whether she wants to deal with you under those circumstances—she might just surprise you.

31. **Lights, Camera, Action!** Erotica can be an exciting added pleasure for some, and for others, a complete and total abomination. Find out your partner's attitude towards sexually explicit materials, before you invite them over to your personal Porno Film Festival. If their displeasure is not due to religious concerns and it's something you really want to share with someone, try introducing it slowly, one step at time and don't just bombard her or him with it all at once. Take a fun trip to the adult video store and pick out something together. Or better yet, make your own erotic video. You may find it exciting, amusing, entertaining and adventurous. All you need is imagination and a camcorder. Don't knock it until you try it.

32. **Ladies, Don't Say** to your lover, **"I'm Going To Give You Some"** or "I'm going to let you have some," men really hate that…(unless you're just kidding of course). It seems to imply that they bring nothing to the table. Remember, you're getting some too! Don't forget, love is a two-way street—but do take turns letting each other drive.

Trying To Cure My Weakness

i don't smoke Cigarettes or Marijuana—
i don't drink Wine, Liquor or Kool Aid—
i don't do
Amphetamines, Barbiturates, Cocaine
Ecstasy, Smack, Crack, Speed
or any of the
Poppy Seed derivatives.
my only WEAKNESS
is Gorgeous Women…
but lately, i've been
EXERCISING, WORKING OUT, LIFTING WEIGHTS
trying to cure my WEAKNESS.

R. Ray Barnes

33. **Guys,** it's a good idea to **Always Dress Nice, Smell Good and Be Neat** and clean—and don't forget the shoes… Make sure your shoes are shined and in good condition. Women truly have a thing about a man's shoes. Just as you like seeing them in sexy shoes, they like seeing you in nice shoes as well—and absolutely no sweat sox with sandals, dress sox with athletic shoes, holey jeans, too long nails, too much or too gaudy jewelry, loud colors, obtrusive patterns and keys hanging from your belt!

Men, you must be mindful, women want from you the same grooming cues that you want and *expect* from them—they're just not as insistent about it. The same thing that turns you on about them, in most cases, are the same things that turn them on regarding you. So, if you admire her feet and hair—then allow her to admire yours. Get manicures and pedicures regularly, keep all your hair well groomed, nose and ears included—trust me, women will truly appreciate you for it!

Again, looks can be deceiving. When a man first meets a woman he may think that not much is going on, as she appears to be just sitting there giving him a polite hello and a smile. On the contrary, in a fairly comprehensive survey, women were found to be doing everything *but* just sitting there being polite; they were sizing the men up from head to toe. According to the *Discovery Science Channel's Megascience* TV show, in an episode that centered around how you look, how you act, and how you attract, they commented, "In a recent experiment, the reactions of 500 young women on their first meeting with a man were recorded and analyzed. The pattern of their eye movement revealed the following: The first 5 seconds she looked into his eyes, but the next 10 her eyes moved up and down the body—first clothes, then taking into account the chest, buttocks and groin. The next 3 seconds focused on the hair and hairline, then an unusually long look at the hands—10 seconds observing things like clean nails, hairy knuckles, a wedding ring, long fingers, interesting gestures then a quick peek at the shoes, a couple of seconds to check if they pass the test. Finally, in the last 15 seconds the pose and the gestures—assessing how he stands and moves. In other words, a comprehensive 45 seconds." So men, you should always be prepared—you have less than a minute to make a good first impression.

In situations where there's a likelihood that you may become intimate with a woman, be sure to wash your hands. It's best to do it in plain sight or in earshot of your prospective lover. She will feel much more comfortable and relaxed *knowing* and not having to *wonder,* whether your hands are clean, before you attempt to let your fingers do the walking around in her precious pink box. It can be awkward and seemingly unromantic for her to have to ask you if your hands are clean.

> ### *Relayshunship*
>
> *I wanna **FUCK** and so do **U**.*
> *So let's get the **FUCKIN'** out of the way*
> *and see whether there can be*
> *anything else 2 our RE-LAY-SHUN-SHIP...*
>
> *Roberto Casanova*

34. **Guys** and **Ladies, Learn To Dress Appropriately** for the occasion. Guys, jeans, shorts, Dockers, Chino pants, Polo shirts, t-shirts, tank tops, sports jerseys, caps and jackets, sweat suits, athletic shoes and sandals are not suitable attire for everywhere she may want you to go.

Immediately destroy any underwear or sox that have holes in them and make sure you have at least two weeks of clean underwear and sox on hand at all times. Plus, find a church or homeless shelter to donate any garments that you haven't worn in a while or that no longer fit properly.

How a man dresses is very sexy to most women and can serve as an aphrodisiac. Even if you don't consider yourself a "suit and tie type of guy," it is a *must* that you own a fine watch and at least one nicely tailored 100 percent wool Italian made suit. In addition, always keep your shoes shined and your hands and feet clean. No exceptions! If you choose to wear open-toe sandals, as mentioned above, get a pedicure. Trust me, it won't kill you nor will it turn you gay. She will love you for it. Women are just as particular about men's feet as guys are about theirs; it's just rarely mentioned or talked about openly.

Although most women usually dress appropriately, when going out, ladies, make sure not to dress *trying* to "be sexy." Remember, sexy is an attitude and a persona, if you have to try to be sexy, then most likely you're not being sexy at all. Work more on dressing sensual and let the sexy part take care of itself. Also, avoid wearing every piece of jewelry you own at the same time—for most, less is best. Lastly, look into a full-length mirror and make sure you're not wearing something that doesn't really fit your body type and style.

35. Save A Tree, But Whack Your Bush. Ladies, trim, cut, shave or do something with your pubic hair to make it look cared for and inviting. You can cut it all off or just leave it natural, but make sure it looks as if it's being maintained and not like a nest for vampire bats. Guys, it's okay for you to trim your hair also. Remember, the longer your pubic hair the more odors it retains. As well, it's not as easy for your lover to perform oral sex, if he or she has to carry a machete.

36. Ladies, If You're Gonna Dress the Part, Then Play the Part. Just as the saying goes, "Clothes alone do not make the man," they can just make the man look good. Neither do clothes alone make a woman sexy. Ladies, you could *own Victoria's Secret* and wear something that makes you *look* sexy every night, but that won't *make* you sexy. Being sexy and looking sexy are two different things. Some women are just born sexy, while others have to work on it. Sexy is an attitude and men love it. Clothes can help you appear sexy, but some of you have to make an effort to *be* sexy. Being sexy begins with how you feel about yourself. You must develop a sense of self-confidence and start seeing yourself as deserving of attention and sexual pleasure.

So if you want to entice your lover, don't just put on erotic clothing or sexy lingerie; wear it, strut it, put it in his face and tease him with it! According to a *Redbook* magazine survey, more than 80 percent of men are turned on when women wear sexy lingerie. So don't be afraid to use what you've got to get what you want.

If you don't know what to wear, make it a fun outing to go shopping and have your lover help you pick something he'd like to see you in. If you're uncomfortable with it at first, try on the outfits and practice by yourself at home until you feel more at ease. You may not become as sexy as Angelina Jolie, Madonna, Marilyn Monroe or Halle Berry overnight, but it can add a little sizzle to your sex life, if you learn how to work it right. The kicker is, you can have lots of fun doing it.

So even when "Prince Charming" is not around, you should still practice dressing sexy for yourself—because you never know who you might meet in your dreams.

37. **Learn How To Give and Receive Compliments.** Compliments are priceless, yet they cost nothing; they're free gifts for you to give at will. Whether you are a cat, a dog, a human or a dolphin, everyone loves to receive sincere compliments. Deepak Chopra, internationally recognized author on the subject of personal and spiritual growth, remarked in his book, *The Seven Spiritual Laws of Success*, "The gifts of caring, attention, affection, appreciation, and love are some of the most precious gifts you can give, and they don't cost you anything."

However, when making compliments be honest and truthful, don't just say what you think someone wants to hear. Also, when complimenting someone, make sure to look him or her in the eye and smile; it adds a sense of sincerity.

As a rule, never disrespect, demean or offend your lover. Don't make sarcastic comments to your lover, then pretend you were kidding and try to switch them to compliments. If you don't have anything positive to say, don't say anything. And don't nag or hassle your lover trying to force or solicit compliments, then express anger if the response isn't what you'd like it to be. If you want honesty and sincerity, you must let the individual convey his or her feelings in one's own manner and time. Try to refrain from blowing your own horn too often and too loudly. If you're always talking and bragging about yourself, your lover may feel there are no compliments left to give—you've already expressed them all.

When receiving compliments, be appreciative. Don't make cynical remarks like, "It's about time you said something nice to me," or "Oh, you finally noticed, huh?" That's a sure way to never get complimented again. If your partner pays you a compliment, an appropriate answer is "thank you," not, "That's what everyone says about me," it seems to belittle the fact that *they* said it.

If your lover (or anyone) compliments you on something that you own or possess, don't respond by telling them how much it cost or what you paid for it. Don't turn their compliment into a boasting and bragging session about you. First, acknowledge the compliment. Then, if appropriate under the circumstances, you may discuss the value or the cost of the item. Sometimes your lover may just want to let you know that they like something that you're wearing and not mean for it to turn it into an episode of the Home Shopping Network or QVC.

Your mother was right! Remember to say 'please' and 'thank you' to your lover. Also, when going on a date to someone's home for the first time, don't go empty-handed; bring something like a bottle of wine or flowers, and don't forget to compliment the host. Gentlemen, be on time for your dates, make it a habit to always open doors for ladies and be sure to call them the day after. Believe it or not, chivalry and basic good manners really do work and will usually pay off in big "appreciation" and "respect" dividends forever.

38. Exercise Your Way To Better Orgasms. With today's mindset of "you get what you pay for," thinking that anything that's worth anything must cost a lot is frightening in a down economy. But did you know that by doing a simple and easy exercise to strengthen a group of your pelvic muscles called the *pubococcygeal (PC) muscle* might provide men and women with a greater number and more pleasurable orgasms? Learning to flex this muscle has proven to add greater sexual sensitivity for both men and women. A strong PC muscle tends to make a woman's vagina tighter and when she squeezes it can give a "gripping" kind of sensation to her partner's penis. Men with toned PC muscles can better control their timing and prolong ejaculation, often adding greater sexual pleasure and satisfaction.

It Doesn't Matter

It doesn't matter... **Yes it does!**
It matters if you say I love you.
It doesn't matter... **Yes it does!**
It matters if you say I look nice today.
It doesn't matter... **Yes it does!**
It matters if you at least try to open the door, pull out the chair.
It doesn't matter... **Yes it does!**
It matters when I speak and you listen as if you really care.
It doesn't matter... **Yes it does!**
It matters when you see a need
and attempt to meet it without being asked...
It does matter how I feel, what I think, what you wear,
where I want to go, what I want to do,
How we make love, fast, quick, and in a hurry
or slow, methodical, passionately, freaky...
It does matter and you need to know,
It matters that I've reached that height we all aspire to,
That peak we all fight and claw for,
Climbing up, falling back, a gash on the head,
a bruise of the heart along the way.
It matters that I count as much as the kids,
the job, the friends, and yes even you do.
It always has – I just didn't know it –
didn't realize how much it mattered to me...
It mattered before and even more so now,
I need it to matter to you
You know, it just should

Denise L. Cook, The Oracle

The exercise itself is an uncomplicated technique first developed in the 1940's by Dr. Arnold Kegel to help his patients with urinary stress incontinence and has now become a popular sex enhancer known as the "Kegel exercise." And best of all, it's free.

The basic concept of the Kegel exercise is to practice tightening your PC muscle as if you were stopping and restarting urination in mid-flow. Many women learn the technique in child birthing class. A good way to begin is to do just that, stop and restart your urine in midstream. When going to the bathroom, try doing about five contractions and releases. If you do this regularly, within the first week you should be able to do it with ease. Thereafter, you can practice without the bathroom; anywhere, any time. In the car at stoplights seems to be a good place or just sitting at your desk at work. At this point, try to hold each muscle contraction longer, about five seconds at first and maybe ten per set. From here your goal should be to increase the amount of time you hold each contraction, maybe even up to 20 seconds per contraction, which many sex therapists have dubbed, the Super Kegel. Eventually, you want to work your way to doing a few hundred Kegels a day. Just don't get crazy with the Kegels too soon, learn to crawl before your walk.

I know for most of you, just the mention of the word exercise can cause heart palpitations. However, in this case the exercise is so easy we've altered the popular phase, "No pain, no gain" to "Mo' gain, no pain." The benefits of doing Kegels are enormous compared to the cost. According to, *SEX: A Man's Guide*, "Women with strong PC muscles say they get sexually aroused more easily, lubricate faster, have more and better orgasms and may achieve orgasm from G-spot stimulation alone. Men who do Kegels find that they have more intense orgasms and sometimes multiple orgasms. It also helps to curb premature ejaculation and it shortens the recovery time between orgasms."

So ladies, if you want to keep it tight, and gentleman if you want to last all night—then you better do your Kegels... all right!

39. **Don't Stop Playing With Toys** just because you're no longer a kid. There is a world of intimate fun and pleasure to be discovered at your local adult sex shop. Another way to achieve better sex is not by opening your legs farther, but by expanding your mind. This should be of special interest to you ladies who find difficulty reaching orgasm. First, stop obsessing and stressing about it; most women fail to achieve orgasm via normal intercourse, as their clitoris is usually not stimulated very much in the process. However, there's help for you at your local sex boutique, where you can find some interesting toys for you and your lover to play with and aid you in reaching climax, (See #59). There you can find things from videos to vibrators, from cock rings to Ben wa balls and everything in between. If you've never been to an adult sex shop, trust me and do yourself a favor; I guarantee you will be overwhelmed with all the toys they offer. No matter how you classify your sexuality: innocent, tame, sensuous, wild, dirty, nasty, way-out, freak of the week, off the chain, homosexual, heterosexual, bisexual, try-sexual, ninety-nine and forty-four one hundreds percent pure, from eighteen to eighty blind cripple or crazy, or whatever…don't worry, they will have something there especially for you.

H. Healthful Hints: Heart Disease and Stroke

If you are in love or plan to be soon, then you're going to need to have a heart in good condition. Love and everything involving love begins and ends with a healthy loving heart, figuratively, romantically and realistically. Roberto says, "One good heart deserves another." So keeping your heart healthy is of utmost importance. And although the effects of losing a relationship may cause a broken heart, no broken heart can match the pain and dangerous effects of "heart disease."

According to the American Heart Association, "Heart disease is the leading killer of Americans today; heart attack is its most visible sign."

The goal is to avoid having a heart attack or stroke. In order to accomplish that, you should make lifestyle choices that can reduce your risk. Some of the major risk factors are: Smoking, High Blood

Pressure, High Cholesterol, Poor Diet and Nutrition, Lack of Physical Activity, Weight Management and Stress. Your family history also plays a part in your risk, as does male sex and age, but your focus needs to be on the risk factors you can alter by changing your attitude and lifestyle.

Karen M. Webster, M.D., MPH, declares, "Our heart muscle is the most important muscle in our bodies and also needs to be exercised regularly. Any commitment to better health (and better sex) should begin with attention to improving our cardiovascular (related to the heart) health. A healthier heart lifestyle should include regular aerobic exercise (an exercise that increases your heart rate to a level which depends on your age and maintains this level for 20-30 minutes 3-5 times per week), a diet which is low in saturated fats and cholesterol, no smoking, and optimal blood pressure and blood glucose control, (especially for those diagnosed with hypertension or diabetes). Consult your personal physician to find out what cardiovascular exercises might be appropriate for your age and current health condition."

To help you acquire and maintain a healthy heart, bodyandfitness.com says, "If you can't get out for a walk or have the time to exercise? Try more sex. During heated lovemaking, your heart rate can reach as high as 130 beats per minute or more." You see, good sex can be good for you!

For more detailed information regarding heart disease, heart attack and stroke, we encourage you to visit the American Heart Association's website at www.americanheart.org.

*Healthful Hints are for information only;
for medical advice see a doctor.*

40. Should You Have Sex On the First Date? Don't worry about someone else's imaginary time line of when it's okay or acceptable to have sex with someone. There is no *magic* number of dates that makes it all right to sleep with someone. Who knows?

In some cases it might be a day, in others it may take months, years or even a lifetime. Some people prefer to wait until they know they're in a committed or exclusive relationship. Others decide to proceed when they know the relationship has long term potential or when they feel they really know one another.

In Iceland it is quite common for women to sleep with men on their first date. I'm not saying it's right or wrong, just informing you that in some cultures it's viewed differently and has no stigma attached to it.

Nevertheless, it should truly be what suits you and your own personal, spiritual, and emotional feelings. The important thing is to make sure that when you decide to sleep with someone it's on your own terms. Be certain that you'll feel all right, regardless of whether he or she calls you the next day. Any sort of time line can only be subjective and whimsical at best. As long as you've taken all the proper safety precautions, don't stress yourself to death worrying about it, just trust your inner feelings. Kahlil Gibran said in his book, *Secrets of the Heart*, "It is wrong to think that love comes from long companionship and preserving courtship. Love is the offspring of spiritual affinity and unless that affinity is created in a moment, it will not be created in years or even generations."

Nonetheless, men should have no expectations of making love on the first date and shouldn't be disappointed if you don't. On the other hand, women should set no *fixed* time limitations; even though you may want to follow your heart, sometimes it may be better to follow your mind. But when seeking sexual driving directions, it's okay for both sexes to follow your hearts, but just not blindly—be sure to keep your *head*lights on at night and during the day!

Love at first sight might be all right—or take your time to make the right find. In either case, don't worry about what your partner may think of you; be more concerned about what you may think of yourself.

Things to Say or Do Before Sex

"Look so sexy in those heels baby, leave 'em on..."

"Just enjoy one another…"

Chapter Four

Things to Say or Do During Sex

You may have gotten this far on your charm and good looks, but now it's time to perform. Remember, 'action speaks louder than words'. However, in your actions be sure to relax and take your time—never rush love. Be sure to be considerate, unselfish and giving. This is the perfect time for realizing and understanding that patience is *truly* a virtue.

> ### Your Love
>
> *If it took all I had to have Your Love…*
> *Your Love would be all I would have.*
>
> *R. Ray Barnes*

41. Always Be Willing To Give More Than You Receive, and be willing to sacrifice your pleasure for the pleasure of your lover. If you're both willing to do those two things, your potential for great lovemaking will be ever present. Just remember, the more you give, the more you will get; and *never* expect to receive more than you are willing to give or deserve. Again, quoting Deepak Chopra, from the Seven Spiritual Laws of Success, "Practicing the *Law of Giving* is actually very simple: if you want joy, give joy to others; if you want love, learn to give love; if you want attention and appreciation, learn to give attention and appreciation; if you want material influence, help others to become materially affluent. In fact, the easiest way to get what you want is to help others get what they want."

So before you begin complaining about what you're *not* getting from your lover or relationship, first take a closer look at yourself and make sure *you're* giving (to your lover) what you think you should be receiving (from your lover). Some people give and *forgive*, while others get and *forget*. Which one are you?

42. **Guys, Sex Is Really *All* About Pleasing Her**. In the *Kundalini Research Institute International Teacher Training Manual Level 1*, it states that, "A man never starts a relationship or ends it of his own accord. Studies have shown that women initiate contact with men over 85 percent of the time by non-verbal or verbal clues. The woman regulates the entire relationship. On the other hand, even her quiet doubting of the relationship can create unrest." The sooner you understand, accept and master that principle, you will *always* have more sex than you can imagine, no matter your age or how you look.

Contrary to popular belief, women aren't nearly as vain as men. Women are much more interested in being loved, cared about and treated special, and are not "hung-up" on age and looks the way many men are. Women are generally much more concerned about how you act toward them than they are about how you look and the material things you possess. Not that looks don't matter to them; it's just not as important as men sometimes think it is. Men must pay closer attention to the often-silent suggestions given by women. When it comes to sex and love, men should learn to follow their lead.

Some men have been led to believe (often by their own egos) that making a woman holler and scream during sex means she's really enjoying it and that he must be the best lover in the world. However, in most cases these men are completely wrong. While there are some women who like to have extremely rough sex, most don't. What some men may have thought to be a command performance, to her may have been quite the opposite. Men must learn to distinguish between moans and groans of pleasure and painful squeals of discomfort.

There is a difference between spirited lovemaking (which most women may enjoy) and trying to intentionally inflict pain. There are some men who really get a kick out of hurting women while having sex, thinking it's some sign of their bravado. The sad part, I think, is that these men don't realize that women can be injured from having sex that is too rough. I've heard one woman describe it as, "He made love to me as if he had just gotten out of prison after several years–that was absolutely no fun for me."

So, guys, make it a habit to ask her how it feels. And women, don't be afraid to express to him how you're truly feeling at the time; if it's painful, insist that he stop! It's imperative that you speak up, because your silence can be interpreted as acceptance. You don't have to be forced to endure unpleasant and uncomfortable sex just to please some man's warped ego. And men, don't be surprised if after an inconsiderate night of lovemaking she never wants to have sex with you again.

Guys, it's okay for you not to have an orgasm every time you have sex, so don't kill her or yourself trying. Remember, "getting her off" is your best insurance policy to keep "getting it on." So my advice: treat her special and keep your sensuous and unselfish love premiums paid-in-full and on time, then she may respond to your claim for sex on time without charging you a deductible.

43. **Never Keep A Lady Waiting** when she's ready and willing to make love to you. Her body is her most precious commodity and you need to appreciate how special she must think you are to be willing to share it with you. So guys, turn off the damn TV! You already have a reputation and a tendency for being "tuned-out" and "insensitive"; don't further exacerbate things by not giving her the proper attention that intimate moments call for and that she deserves.

So before you begin to make love to her, turn off the basketball game, the football game, the baseball game, soccer, hockey, boxing, *ESPN, Sports Center, the Best Damn Sports Show Period, Sports Century, Around the Horn, Pardon the Interruption, The X Games, Beyond the Glory, the Golf Channel, the Speed Channel, The Sports List, Fox Sports News, CNN Sports Illustrated, the Outdoor Channel, American Outdoorsman, the Fishing Channel, Rome Is Burning, NBA Inside Stuff, NBA 2Night, RPM 2Night, Totally NASCAR, NHL Tonight, Baseball Tonight, Rodeo Roundup, Cold Pizza,* etc., and all those other damn sports shows that rerun several times a day. Turn it off and just *record* it. Try soft music and candles instead.

For the precious few minutes you may have, pleasing your lover should be your *only* focus and concern. With the way women have been complaining recently, most of you men will have plenty of time to watch TV. Besides, according to a January 18, 2006 CNN report of an Italian study, "Couples who didn't have TVs had twice as much sex as those who did." So, men, attend to your beautiful woman and satisfy *her* needs. Because if you don't—somebody else will! You can consider that a promise, a threat or just the stone cold truth!

44. For most lovemaking occasions, it's best to **Always Be Clean, Smell Good, and Have Fresh Breath;** unless it's just one of those times when you're hot and sweaty and you both understand. Otherwise, take full showers and baths and don't just wash-up or take "bird-baths."

Most men and women, especially in newer relationships, usually won't tell their partners if they have body odor—they often just endure it or avoid any close and personal contact rather than chance the embarrassment of talking about it. We all have a natural body aroma that is uniquely ours; however, if possible be sure to check yourself to make sure you are fresh before any intimate or sexual encounters. From our interviews with several women, many said they use the simple "vagina finger test," to check for any unusual smells or odors. It may not be a bad idea for men to use self-examination techniques to detect any unnatural manly scents also.

Unless you both smoke, try to avoid smoking on your dates and while you're being intimate. At the very least, ask your partner if you desire to smoke.

9. Healthful Hints: Smoking and Sex

We are all probably well aware of the dangers of cigarette smoking as it relates to our general health. The United States Department of Health & Human Services asserts that smoking shortens lives by about 14 years and is the leading cause of cancer fatalities. But few of us seem aware of how it may affect our ability to perform sexually. A quoted survey within the article, Smoking Can Harm Your Sexual Health, by the mega pharmaceutical giant GlaxoSmithKline, states that, "…most people find smoking a drag when considering a romantic partner, with more than three-quarters of adults preferring to date non-smokers."

The survey also indicated that smoking can have a serious effect on a man's sexual performance noting that, "Smoking restricts blood flow and can impact the quality of sexual response. In one study, smokers as young as 31-49 were 50% more likely than nonsmokers to report and suffer from erectile dysfunction."

Our own Karen M. Webster, M.D., MPH emphasizes that, "There is no question that smoking indirectly causes more deaths in the U.S. than HIV, drug abuse, and cancer. Heart disease, stroke, lung cancer, bladder cancer, esophageal cancer, cervical cancer, all have direct links to cigarette smoking. Nicotine is definitely addictive! The best thing ANY smoker can do to extend his or her life or enhance one's current quality of their life is to stop smoking. There are good helpful aids available from your doctor that in combination with counseling and medical support are very effective. And just because you did not succeed in quitting when you tried in the past, does not mean you will not succeed this time."

Dr. Cheryl Healton, President/CEO of the American Legacy Foundation said in an interview on Good Morning America on April 18, 2005, "Nicotine is well understood to be the most addictive substance known to humankind..." Again, on January 31, 2009 on the NBC Today Show, Dr. Healton added, "It is important to understand how strong that addiction is and to know that it is ok to seek help to quit smoking." And agreeing with Dr. Webster, she continued: "You should not be demoralized if on the first time out you don't succeed. It's a desperately difficult thing to do...but it is the most important thing you can do for your health, bar anything."

And according to the website MatchMaker.com, "Everyday smoking could be another reason for dampening the sexual desire because the nicotine in cigarettes can cause arteries to constrict and reduce blood flow to the vaginal area. Less blood flow to the vaginal area means less sensitivity in your genitalia, which may make it more difficult to become aroused and achieve orgasm."

Moreover, for couples thinking about having children, the United States Surgeon General reports that, "smoking during pregnancy increases the risk of pregnancy complications, premature delivery, low-birth-weight infants, stillbirth, and sudden infant death syndrome (SIDS)."

For more detailed information on the dangers of smoking, we encourage you to visit the American Lung Association's website at www.Lungusa.org or United States Department of Health & Human Service's website at www.hhs.gov, under Safety and Wellness.

*Healthful Hints are for information only;
for medical advice see a doctor.*

45. **Your Mind Is On Vacation** and your mouth is working overtime. Guys, you sometimes sound like "Mynah birds," that can say the words but haven't a clue *what* they're saying. Try not to do or say anything more than what's necessary to accomplish your desired goals with women, be it sexual or otherwise.

Men, in particular, have been known to talk their way into some fantastic sexual situations with women, but, because they wouldn't shut-up, they'd soon discover they had talked themselves right out of it. When a beautiful woman has given you the "green light," you must *go* immediately or she may give you a ticket (for impeding the flow) at a price you *can't* afford. So remember, a green light only stays green for so long, with a little caution, it quickly turns red again.

Ladies and gents, try to avoid repeated conversations about past lovers, unless it's used in some positive or enlightening way to benefit your present relationship. Any comparisons should be to show how your current relationship is better; if not, don't mention it. As a rule, most people don't want to hear about how wonderful your "ex" was. Besides, if your ex was so wonderful, why aren't you still together? Remember, it's hard to discover a future love if a past love occupies your present.

46. **Sometimes You Have "Sex,"** sometimes you **"F#@k,"** and sometimes you **"Make Love."** Always know which one you're supposed to be doing and act accordingly. Men, you need to pay special attention to this! You don't want to be in the right place at the wrong time—doing the "foxtrot" when you should be doing the "twist" or the "cool jerk."

Moreover, be careful not to use sex as a stress reliever. In *Tantric Secrets, 7 Steps To The Best Sex Of Your Life*, it states, "Some couples use sex as a way of releasing tension, but this is a waste of the potential riches that good lovemaking can bring. Conversely, too much stress may put you off sex all together. If you are carrying tension in your body, you need to release it before sex rather than during sex. You can't hope to access sexual bliss if you are using sex to deal with the build-up of stress in your system." It further says, "…you need to deal with the tension in your body before lovemaking, rather than rely on your partner to give you release through orgasm. Your partner is probably just as stressed as you are."

Nevertheless, the act of lovemaking, especially along with intimate foreplay can be very relaxing. So if one partner or the other is feeling very stressed, try to relieve the stress with scented candles, soft music, a hot bath and a body massage before making love.

47. **Guys,** in most cases, **Don't Be In Such A Hurry.** As we mentioned earlier in #24, take your time. Unless she suggests you move at a quicker pace, slow it down. Or, unless it's just one of those rare special moments when you're both so anxious you just can't wait.

Many men miss out on more sex by trying to rush into it and being impatient with her. Women are peculiar creatures, who often change their minds in a heartbeat. She may have started the evening convinced that she was going to make love to you, until you decided you couldn't wait for her to feel secure in her decision, which prompted her to change her mind. Remember, there's no need to rush; you're not trying to extinguish a fire—you're trying to get one started. Just take your time, rub your two little sticks together until you get a spark.

When you think of lovemaking, imagine yourself as a Master Chef cooking up some sweet juicy love in a Crock-Pot instead of a microwave. As with slow cooking, when you approach lovemaking slowly, you have time to add more sexual spices and seasonings along the way, making the love moist, tender, succulent and more aromatic; unleashing love's true flavor. In contrast, fast cooking at high temperatures make the meats less juicy and more salty, which similarly to her hurried lovemaking, will tend to result in your partner's attitude being dry, salty and less flavorful.

So, don't be hasty with her. Just wait until she feels comfortable and she will reward you for your patience and understanding.

48. **Guys, As A Rule, Be Gentle…**unless she indicates that she wants you to be rough. Be sure to understand that the woman is the "tender gender." Thus, on most occasions and most of the time, it may prove best for you to treat her in a tender way—in word, in deed, and inside her vagina. In other words, be nice to her kitty and her kitty may be nice to you. Just remember, though a pussycat may have nine lives, a woman has only *one* kitty.

J. Healthful Hints: High Blood Pressure

Julie says, "Good health makes good sex even better," but it's hard to have good low-down, no holds barred sex if you have hypertension, commonly known as "high blood pressure. High blood pressure affects your heart, and anything that affects your heart— affects how you love.

In November 2008, the National Heart Lung and Blood Institute (NHLBI) of the National Institutes of Health (NIH) reported that approximately 72 million people in the United States, which is about 1 in 3 adults, has high blood pressure. It's prevalence seems to increase with age as males over 45 and females over 55 are at greater risk for high blood pressure, which can lead to coronary heart disease, heart failure, stroke, kidney failure and other health problems.

According to the American Heart Association, "High blood pressure (or hypertension) is defined in an adult as a blood pressure greater than or equal to 140 mm Hg systolic pressure or greater than or equal to 90 mm Hg diastolic pressure.

High blood pressure is particularly prevalent in African Americans, middle-aged and elderly people, obese people, heavy drinkers and women who are taking birth control pills. In 90 to 95 percent of high blood pressure cases, the cause is unknown. In fact, you can have high blood pressure for years without knowing it. That's why it's the "silent killer" — it creeps up on you. Don't let high blood pressure creep up on you. Get your blood pressure checked regularly. Just remember, if you take good care of your heart… your heart will take good care of you!

For more information regarding the dangers of high blood pressure, visit the American Heart Associations website, www.americanheart.com and the National Heart Lung and Blood Institute (NHLBI) of the National Institutes of Health, www.nhlbi.nih.gov.

*Healthful Hints are for information only;
for medical advice see a doctor.*

49. **If It Don't Fit, Don't Force It.** Guys, women are very different as to the time it takes for them to become sexually aroused. If you find she's not wet or lubricated, you should be very understanding, because more than likely it's on you. As we stated in #9, you may not be making her feel relaxed or comfortable enough; so don't rush her; be patient and remember the importance of intimate foreplay. She could also be having second thoughts about her desire to have sex with you, so make no motion towards sex unless she's given you the proper "e-motion."

When you're certain she wants to have sex with you and she's still not lubricated, instead of running your mouth complaining about it, you should use your mouth and tongue to do something about it.

Rainy Afternoon

On this
Rainy Afternoon
I Miss **You** the most.
The **"intimate"** fun we could share
if only you were here...
So, instead,
I play with my imagination...
trying to recapture
some of the moments we've shared—
but,
On this
Rainy Afternoon
nothing can make me
wet—
except,
Your Smile
Your Touch
Your Love...

Bianca Baker / R. Ray Barnes

Things to Say or Do During Sex 103

50. **During Lovemaking Learn To Listen** and pay close attention to your lover's silent hints and suggestions, then act upon them.

51. **Shut-Up Already and Listen!** Be careful about what you say, and stop talking loud and saying nothing. If you have nothing meaningful to say, then be quiet. Learn to listen and pay attention! As we've previously stated, say what you mean and mean what you say. Don't be afraid to let your lover know what you want and desire. Direct your lover to the spot. Guide his or her hands, if necessary, and say "yes that's it," "I love it when you touch me there," "try putting it here," "harder," "softer," etc. Don't make assumptions—know for sure by asking them. "Do you like it like this?" "Does this feel good?" "What would you like me to do?"

Communication is the most important ingredient of *any* relationship. In *The Four Agreements*, Don Miguel Ruiz states, "With clear communication, all of your relationships will change, not only with your partner, but with everyone else." Where there is only a little communication and understanding, there can only be a little love. So men, 'If you don't speak now, you may be forever holding your piece.'

"Shower each other with love..."

> ## Now Hear This!
>
> *you seem always to*
> **Hear**
> *everything i say...*
> *and on most occasions you can quote me,*
> *-time and date*
> *-word for word*
> *-phrase for phrase...*
> *however, you seem never to really*
> **Listen.**
>
> — *R. Ray Barnes*

Remember, as mentioned before, communication is not always verbal; a great deal of how we communicate with each other sexually is silent. So don't only listen to what your lover says, but watch closely and tune into what he or she is feeling and expressing.

With most of the couples we interviewed, clear and effective communication was cited as the number one reason they stayed together. Whereas lack of clear and effective communication was the number one reason couples felt their relationships failed. Needless to say, communication seems to be the hinge on which the door swings that allows us to enter into the realm of successful relationships. In *Tantric Secrets, 7 Steps To The Best Sex Of Your Life*, it addresses communication in this fashion, "Use open communication to create harmony and purpose in your sexual relationship. This means speaking your truth and being heard, but remaining open and willing to hear the truth of others. Make communication real; don't fake it. You don't need to fake anything you don't feel. The key to real power is authenticity." So when feelings, gestures, statements or other issues arise with your partner that you don't understand or are unclear about, you should always make it a habit to discuss the matter, before the

Things to Say or Do During Sex

"Often times silence speaks louder than words..."

matter becomes *disgusting* to you. According to *Ultimate Sex*, author Judy Bastyra says, "COMMUNICATION IS KEY even in the shortest relationships—it is important that you let the other person know what you are expecting. This is not just to avoid misunderstandings, but also in order to get what you want."

Here are a few suggestions that may help you communicate more effectively with your lover. Remember, sex may be a door to a relationship, but communication is the key that opens that door to love.

A, B, C's
To Better Communication

A. *Don't lie! Be truthful and sincere. Don't judge or try to control; completely accept your partner as he or she is.*

B. *Be free to express your feelings, but speak from your heart, not your ego. Try to make your words temperate and courteous, not harsh and criticizing. Be enthusiastic; yet, avoid shouting, name-calling and using foul or insulting language—a sharp tongue often cuts its own throat.* **Never** *resort to verbal or physical abuse!*

C. *When confronted verbally, don't lose control and blurt out a response. Think swiftly like the hare; speak slowly and deliberately like the tortoise. In other words, be quick to assess the situation and process your thoughts, but take your time when you articulate them, so that your answer is rational and coherent and not merely an emotional outburst.*

D. *When having open conversations with your partner, avoid using personal examples where you can be perceived to be the positive one in the example, and your partner perceived as the negative one. When you do, it often leads to retaliation, personal attacks, hurt feelings, defensive posturing or may just cause your partner to shut down. Instead, try to keep the conversation general, focusing* on the principle of the point you want to illuminate and not on what you would do personally. Then, if absolutely necessary, for further clarity and understanding, you may use honest personal examples.

E. Ladies, many men fear that if they get into a serious conversation with you it will go on forever, so when attempting to talk to men (especially about issues of love and intimacy) it may be very helpful to agree to a time restraint prior to beginning (and abide by it); then he may be more willing to talk, knowing that the conversation will not go on indefinitely.... However, if and when your partner agrees to talk, you must be patient and listen to his responses. Don't cut him off in anticipation of his reply. Relax and let him talk. Maybe you'll get a better understanding of how he truly feels. Remember, you aren't learning much when your lips are moving.

Men, ladies often complain that you talk over them, so you may try allowing each other to speak uninterrupted for 10 to 15 minutes, withholding any comments until afterward—but when doing so, you must be attentive. This will make it possible for each of you to express yourself, complete your thoughts and be heard without anyone dominating the conversation.

F. Don't use knowledge or information you've gained from your lover in trust as evidence against them later.

G. If at all possible, get in the habit of answering questions with a, "yes" or "no" before you begin a dissertation trying to explain why you're avoiding just answering the question yes or no. If an explanation or justification is required or needed, try doing so after you first answer the question.

H. Before getting into a debate with your partner, try to see the issue from his or her point of view, prior to forming your final opinion. After starting your car, you must apply the brakes before you can put the car in any gear to drive; utilize that same safety principle with your partner. Stop! Apply the brakes first and put your mind in gear, *before you drive your partner into an argument. If it still happens that you disagree with your partner's opinion, don't just totally disregard his or her feelings by attacking them head on. Soften your response by agreeing with them first. For example say: "Honey, I see how you could feel that way; however...." or, "I understand how it may appear like that to you, but...." and, "Honey, I think you may be right when you look at it from that point of view, yet, when you look at it from this perspective...." Moreover, remember, never allow a minor dispute to injure a major love relationship or friendship.*

I. *When mistakes are made in your relationship, don't focus on 'who's to blame', concentrate on the solution. Don't be afraid to admit mistakes that you've made and to accept the responsibility for them. When admitting a mistake, take immediate steps to correct it. If an explanation is needed, give reasons (be they right or wrong); however, avoid way-out stories, blaming others, and lame excuses.*

J. *Learn to apologize and say, "I'm sorry," and mean it, with no ifs, ands, buts, or justifications about it! And when saying "I'm sorry," show that you are sincere by looking your partner in the eye. If the situation permits, try to apologize as soon as possible after the transgression, it may prevent any build-up of resentment. Having done those things, one day when you're deserving of an apology, your lover may be willing to apologize to you. However, if you are found guilty of lying, cheating, and any deceitful behavior, you must realize that trust (in you) has been compromised and must be **earned** again, before it can be restored. So even after having apologized, don't expect the injured party to heal overnight. Forgiveness is easier said than done. Don't rush the recovery; show in a caring and loving way that you understand the restoration of trust and the healing process may take a little time.*

K. *Be willing to forgive your lover, realizing that it may take some time to 'get over it'. However, once you have forgiven your partner (although you may not forget), you must 'let it go' and not continue to use the forgiven transgression against him or her.*

L. Don't make it a habit to complain about the things you don't like. Try, instead, talking more about what you would prefer. As an example, don't say, "I hate it when you kiss me on my earlobes." Rather than complaining, be encouraging by saying, for example, "Baby, why don't you kiss me on my neck, I love it when you kiss me there."

M. If you don't like the style of clothing your partner wears, don't make distasteful remarks about it. Instead, be proactive and buy something you'd like to see him or her wear; then let your lover see how much better the new outfit looks. You can also use this approach for many things other than clothes.

N. Don't set up your partner in a "no win" situation by asking for advice or input on something you've already made up your mind about and are not **truly** open to other points of view; then get angry if your partner doesn't agree with you. In other words, don't ask for input when you know that your partner's opinion or advice won't really matter unless it agrees with yours. Instead, just inform your lover of the decision you've made.

O. Ladies: Someone once asked the question why it takes a million sperm to find one egg; the answer: because like men, they never stop to ask for directions. For some God forsaken reason men hate to be given advice regarding directions.

So when it comes to giving a man directions, if you don't want to get lost or be driven hundreds of miles out of the way, this may be the one time it might prove beneficial to pretend to be the stereotypical 'dumb blonde' or helpless female. When you know he's going the wrong way, try approaching him like this: "Honey, I think the map is saying we should be going the other way, but you know I don't know how to read these things as well as you, so, sweetheart, would you please stop and take a look at this map for me and show me the way we really should be going." Ladies remember, in most cases, men must have their egos fed before they can think properly.

P. Men: Believe it or not, women actually realize that you don't know the answer to everything. So, there is no shame in admitting that you don't know the correct answer to something, as opposed to concocting what you may think sounds like a clever answer, which in most cases (even though she may not call you on it) sounds to her exactly like you don't know what the hell you're talking about! Trust me, she knows a lot more than you think or give her credit for. Note: You can put lipstick on a pig, but it's still a hog.

Q. Men: When you ask a woman, "What's wrong?" and she answers, "Nothing," it usually means everything is wrong and you're probably at fault or to blame. So, guys, put your boots on 'cause you're almost certainly going to be in some deep s#*%. But ladies, if you're saying 'nothing's wrong' just to get him to react, don't be surprised if he takes your word for it and doesn't respond and actually acts as if there's nothing wrong.

R. Men: When a woman says, "Well just go ahead and do it then," don't be fooled into believing that she means for you to proceed; she really means the exact opposite. It's actually a dare and a dire warning that if you do 'go ahead and do it' you'll need your boots again; except this time you may need your pillow, blankets and a doghouse, too.

S. Ladies: When a man says, "Well just F#@k-it then..." or "I don't have to stand here and listen to this..." It usually means he's guilty and you've caught him in a situation that he can't get out of. In other words, his excuses, explanations and usual tactics to try to convince you of his innocence have failed.

T. Men: When a woman says, "Whatever!" It usually means that she really doesn't give a damn what you do at this point. Or, in the extreme case, it's just a nice way for her to say, "F#@k you!"

U. Ladies: When a man stutters while attempting to answer a question and he doesn't have a speech impediment, it's usually a sign that he's not being completely forthright, that he's lying, covering up something or, at worst, he's guilty.

V. Men: When a woman says, "Okay fine!" It really doesn't mean that things are fine at all. Don't make the mistake of presuming that she's in some way admitting defeat or that you're right. It's just a way of saying she's tired of discussing the issue or continuing the argument at that time and she needs to gather more ammunition. So don't relax or rest on your laurels; the matter will definitely be revisited again real soon—so take cover, make plans for a good defense or be prepared to mount a powerful offense…because, trust me, she's coming back with a vengeance and it's not going to be pretty.

W. Ladies: Men are not mind readers or clairvoyant and don't have extra sensory perception—quite the contrary; most men have very little insight into things you may want or need done. So, if you really want them to do something in particular, don't give them subtle hints, strong hints, or obvious hints—just say what you want them to do!

X. Men: When a woman says, "That's okay, don't worry about it!" It usually means that she's fed up with you and you should worry like hell about it. In most cases, it indicates that she's asked you several times to do something, perform some task, answer some questions and you have yet to do it. Don't try to explain or attempt to engage her in some clever discourse trying to bulls#*% your way out of it. It's really best that you get it done, before she gets it done on her own–or the next thing you hear from her may be, "Whatever!" in the extreme case.

Y. Never miss a good chance to shut-up. Because the more your mouth is closed, the less chance you'll have of putting your foot in it! It has been said that God gave us two ears but only one mouth. Maybe he was trying to suggest that we should listen twice as much as we speak.

Z. Men: I read somewhere that there are two theories to arguing with women—and I would share them with you, however, neither one works!

Make an effort in *all* of your loving relationships to strive for open, honest and effective communication. Express yourself clearly with *understanding* being your ultimate goal; not determining who's right and who's wrong. Endeavor to go beyond that uncomfortable place where we hide when it comes to revealing and sharing our most intimate feelings.

However, notwithstanding anything to the contrary, it's not always easy trying to communicate with women about sex. In *SEX: A Man's Guide*, the popular syndicated columnist Ann Landers observed, "Women complain about sex more often than men. Their gripes fall into two major categories: not enough and too much," so go figure.

> ## *Silent Conversations*
>
> *i am learning to*
> ***Speak** with my **Mind**...*
> *without my mouth*
> *without words*
> *without gestures*
> *without smoke signals*
> *without drums*
> *without sound...*
> *noiseless, hush, quiet*
> *Just Silence...*
> *i hope you're learning to*
> ***Listen** and **Understand**.*
>
> *R. Ray Barnes*

52. **Be Spontaneous and Creative,** like the song by Quincy Jones featuring James Ingram, which says, *"Find One Hundred Ways."* Don't do the same thing, in the same order, in the same way all the time. Strive to make your lovemaking an imaginative adventure and not let it become a boring habit. Dress-up, role-play and play sex games with your partner. Tease each other. Don't always give-it-up or give-in too easily. Also, you don't have to confine your lovemaking to the bedroom or the four walls inside your home. Anywhere should be open for consideration, just use discretion and common sense. In the daylight is all right or in the park after dark can really be fun, erotic and enjoyable, but you must be aware of and take into consideration the public decency laws where you may be, so you don't cause yourself more problems than pleasure.

We've all heard the saying, "Variety is the spice of life," and that goes for sex, too. So try adding a bit of sensuality to your sex life. Make use and incorporate all of your five senses when making love. *Touch* softly with your fingertips and use different textures such as silks, satins, velvet, leathers, feathers, rubber, soft brushes, erotic gloves and your own hands and fingernails to enhance your sexual experience. Whatever your musical taste, try adding that *Sound* to your love mix. Remember the old adage, "What you *See* is what you get;" so light your way into a beautiful loving experience. Use candles, soft lights, tea lights, nightlights and the sensuous flicker of fireplace lighting to create the right visual atmosphere. Fragrance is a multi-billion dollar a year business and that's for good reason. We all like things that *Smell* good, so, whether you prefer

"Thank you for being there for me…"

real flowers, potpourri, incense, scented oils or candles, don't be afraid to spend a couple dollars to make the aroma therapeutic for making love. Now speaking of *Taste*, the best taste is the unadulterated taste of sex itself. Tasting the natural juices that's him and the natural juices that's her. I know we all think the vagina and the penis are most important when it comes to lovemaking. However, in *SEX, A Man's Guide*, it says, "The tongue is your most versatile sex organ. You can touch with it, taste with it, lick with it." So let's not take our tongues and taste for granted. You may add to the taste sensation with some warm chocolate or butterscotch, the juiciness of your favorite fruit, the soft texture of whipped cream and the coldness of ice cream.

> ### Silent Night...
>
> *after u rubbed me down in oils,*
> *we began making* **Love**—
> *on the floor in front of the fireplace.*
> *i didn't say much & neither did u...*
> *but i heard u loud and clear & i guess u heard me 2—*
> *because we changed positions...*
> *& i came & so did u.*
>
> *R. Ray Barnes*

Also, try being sexually creative and learn how to master more than the missionary position. Be playful and not so serious all the time. Sex should be exciting and enjoyable, not a chore. Experiment. Don't be afraid to take risks and have sex in odd places at unusual times. Remember, humans are the only species who have sex and procreate while facing each other. So, from time to time, open your eyes and look at your lover. There is a hidden world of passion and emotion revealed in one's eyes. The eyes are the windows of the soul—looking into your lover's eyes while making love can make the sexual experience a great deal more pleasurable.

If you find yourself away from your lover for any extended periods of time, phone sex may be a good way to keep the fire burning, or try a little lap dance with your laptop and enter the realm of cyber sex. Also try an exotic hotel as a getaway.

When you're in a committed loving relationship, you mustn't be afraid to become a "try-sexual." Yes! That means being willing to *try* anything to please your lover.

K. Healthful Hints: Premature Ejaculation

According to AskMen.com, in an article titled, Tips For Curing Premature Ejaculation, *by D. Zimmer, it states that, "Although premature ejaculation is the most common sexual dysfunction, it is very difficult for men to discuss. A man who 'can't get it up' or keep it up, understandably feels like less of a man. However, it should not be this way. If more men were willing to talk about their problem, it would be easier to accept, knowing that they are not alone.*

Often, men are not sure what is considered premature ejaculation. The average male takes less than 3 minutes from the time of insertion till he ejaculates. According to the technical definition, it is ejaculation that occurs prior to when a man wishes, or too quickly during intercourse to satisfy the partner.

The complaint of premature ejaculation is usually stated in terms of time, this is because it is the only way to measure and compare. One man might feel proud to last ten minutes, while this may be too short for another.

The good news is that this is a problem that is highly curable, providing the man is willing to get help and invest the time and effort needed. It is believed that 80-90% of men are able to learn better control through therapy."

For more detailed information on how to avoid and control premature ejaculation, we encourage you to visit, www.AskMen. com and www.sexhealth.org.

---

*Healthful Hints are for information only;
for medical advice see a doctor.*

Can't Find The Words...

Dear Sweetheart,
I have something very important I need to tell you...
however,
I don't know exactly how to say it.
It's rather difficult for me to express the way I feel,
and
I just can't figure out the best way to phrase it.
I certainly don't want to alarm you
but,
It's been keeping me up nights and
my sense of honesty dictates that I must say something,
however,
I can't quite find the proper words.
*You see, I don't want to be **too** blunt,*
although,
I do want you to feel the full impact of what I have to say.
I hope you understand that I truly do care about your feelings,
and
I do want to voice this the right way.
yet,
I can't seem to make up my mind how to tell you.
I'm totally at a loss for words.
I really don't know how I should put it.
As you can tell this is not very easy for me.
I am sincerely having a hard time with this whole thing—
It has indeed become quite perplexing.
so,
I hope you will please forgive me for writing it down like this
and
Not just coming right out and telling you—
FACE to FACE, PERSON to PERSON...

> ***nonetheless**,*
> *I must admit, I just don't have the nerve—*
> ***and***
> *The last thing I want to do is shock you by simply blurting it out!*
> ***however**,*
> *I guess I really don't have a choice...*
> *I'm just going to have to take a deep breath,*
> *bite the bullet and go ahead and break the news.*
> *I just pray you can handle*
> *what I have to say without over-reacting—*
> *Well, here goes—Baby, Sweetheart, Darling...*
> *When It **Comes** To Loving Me You're Just **So Damn Good**!!!*
>
> *R. Ray Barnes*

L. Healthful Hints: Erectile Dysfunction

Erectile dysfunction (sometimes referred to as impotence) is the recurrent inability of a man to obtain or sustain an erection sufficient for satisfying sexual intercourse. Dr. Webster advises us that most men experience this to some degree at some point in their lives. It is estimated that 5% of men experience this by age 40, and 15-25% experience this by age 65. This problem is most often due to diseases such as diabetes, hardening of the arteries, kidney disease, alcoholism and other abnormalities that affect the nervous system or blood vessels (including smoking).

Certain medications used to treat high blood pressure or depression may also cause erectile dysfunction and certainly psychological disorders or stress may be contributory. This condition may create difficulties within an otherwise healthy relationship as well as lead to self-doubt, decreased interest in sex, and low self esteem. Although this is often a very sensitive and even embarrassing condition to discuss with your doctor, most often this condition is treatable and the pleasures of satisfying sex can be restored with oral medicines such as Viagra, Levitra and Cialis, penile implants or vacuum devices. Don't let potential embarrassment prevent you from seeking help, and remember that medications are to be used only by the person they are prescribed for—let your doctor decide what treatment might be best for you.

According to AskMen.com, "When just a single incident occurs, the best thing to do is forget about it. There is no reason for a man to worry about something that almost all men experience a few times in their lives. Problems arise when this difficulty starts occurring regularly. Men afflicted with repeated impotence tend to be middle-aged and older, with the condition most common in men 60 years of age and older. Regardless of the age, many men who have this problem can be treated successfully.

Impotence results from a wide variety of problems. As with any other ailment, when a person begins having this problem repeatedly, he needs to see a doctor."

For more detailed information regarding erectile dysfunction, we encourage you to visit, www.AskMen.com and the American Academy of Physicians website, at www.familydoctor.org.

*Healthful Hints are for information only;
for medical advice see a doctor.*

53. Tell Your Lover You Care About Her or Him and make your lover feel special. Remember, you don't have to be *in love* with someone to make this person feel special or to say you care about her or him; it *will* make a difference. Kindness has a way of making any situation feel better. Although it may be a "one night stand" a "fling" or just a "f#@k," most people don't want to feel that way about it… especially women.

54. **Guys, If You Have A Bout of Premature Ejaculation**, don't blame her, don't make excuses, and don't just turn over and forget about her. As soon you get wind that you have ejaculated sooner than desired, move quickly; don't wait for it to become an issue. Find other ways to satisfy her—you'll be glad you did and so will she. This is a good opportunity for some of you to put that big mouth of yours to good use—or for you creative bad boys to play with your toys.

If premature ejaculation is a common problem for you, Dr. Judith Kuriansky, clinical psychologist and sex therapist, in an article appearing in *The Big Black Book*, says, "The answer to this problem lies in learning to control the timing of ejaculation. This is easier than you think. You have to find the point at which you can no longer stop yourself from ejaculating. During masturbation, practice ways in which you can decrease or increase feelings of arousal. Discover which fantasies or behavior triggers your excitement and what diminishes it, and learn how to focus on the latter in order to postpone ejaculation."

55. **Ladies, Don't Complain If Your Lover "Can't Get It Up."** Just be mindful of what you say and try to be of some help. Lie on his chest and be silently supportive. Don't say *anything* like, "That's all right baby, it'll be better next time." Or, "I know that happens to all men at times," etc. The less you say is best. The more you remind him of it, the worst he will feel.

Sometimes oral or hand stimulation can help, but not always. However, if it's one of those times when oral or hand stimulation won't work, then it just may exacerbate the situation. So in most cases, it's best to take your clues from him as to what you should do. He may not express himself very openly about it, so pay close attention to his silent suggestions. Mainly, you just want to try to relax him. Give him a massage and talk about other things—you might just be surprised. But remember guys, if your big boy doesn't want to deploy, use a toy.

56. **A Winner Never Quits and A Quitter Never Wins.** Never complain about how long it takes for your lover to become satisfied. Just try to encourage each other to reach his or her peak. This is not always so easy for women. Women have been complaining since the dawn of man about the difficulty they have in reaching orgasm. According to Ph.D., sex therapist and psychology professor at the University of Utah in Salt Lake City, Donald Strassberg, "Men need to learn that women are very different from one another—much more so than men. For men pretty much anything works. Apply some friction to his penis and he's happy. Women, on the other hand, become aroused in different places on the body; they respond to different levels of stimulation, different tempos. And they are even variable from one time to the next."

So ladies, as mentioned before, communication can be very helpful at times like these. We know men don't like taking directions from women while driving, but in the bed it's different. So help direct your lover to the right places, so that you reach your destination on time.

Guys, remember what we said in #41, "Be willing to sacrifice your pleasure for the pleasure of your lover." Moreover, try holding off your orgasm until she reaches hers, and don't waste your time using your mouth to complain about how long she may take when you should be using your mouth to do something about it (See #59). Understanding, patience, sacrifice and giving are some of the major bricks that are used in building a strong relationship. So take whatever time necessary to please her. Patience is a virtue. If you plan to keep making love to her, rest assured you're going to eventually need her to be patient with you; so just keep trying, because a winner never quits and a quitter never wins.

Nutcracker Sweet

Love may seem a Hard & Bitter Nut to Crack...
But, once you get inside and savor it's Sweet & Tender Meat—
It'll have you Cumming & Going...

Julie Lovelace

57. Do each other a favor... **Ladies,** sometimes **Give Him A Quickie, and Guys,** sometimes **Go As Long As She Wants You To**, or vice versa—with no complaints from either of you.

Further, in your effort to please her, remember, she's a soft, sensitive and gentle creature who would like to be treated that way most of the time. As we have repeatedly stated, learn to take your time! I read somewhere to pretend that her body is a source of hidden treasures. Whereupon, there is a wonderful cache of gold and jewels hidden (or better yet, the TV remote), and you must explore every nook and cranny of her body; searching (her mouth, her lips, her ear lobes, behind her ears, her neck, her hair, her arms, her hands, her breast, her navel, the fold of her back, her butt, her thighs, behind her knees, that spot below her calf and above her ankle, her feet and her toes) with your hands and tongue, until you finally discover that the gold and jewels are hidden inside her vagina.

Likewise, for you ladies, don't always wait for him to be the one to suggest or initiate a quickie. Be spontaneous, creative, and inventive. Break the weekends and nights only sex routine that's easy to slip into when you have a family and demanding jobs and just raise your skirt and invite him to creep up behind you for some unexpected sexual fun in the kitchen, the bathroom or on the living room floor. In the book *Ultimate Sex*, it states, "Seizing the moment and surprising each other with unplanned flurries of passion keeps excitement and desire alive, adding spice and maintaining the longevity of the relationship.

Quickie sex is a wonderfully erotic and lustful way of adding diversity to your love life. Although it cannot and should not replace the long sensual hours of foreplay and lovemaking that are essential in all loving and respectful relationships, it has its place, reaffirming each other's sexuality and reassuring your partner that you still find [him or her] the sexiest and most desirable person on the planet. Variety is not described as the spice of life without good reason."

The impromptu quickie can also serve as a way to convey to your lover that the thrill is not gone and to reiterate your love and desire for each other.

Although men tend to want more quickies than women, and women tend to want to savor the flavor much more than men, when it comes down to love, in most cases, it's like the old folks use to say, "What's good for the goose is good for the gander." But on occasion, whichever way your partner prefers to make love—like Nike says, "Just Do It!"

> ## Yes! Right There
>
> *what bliss*
> *sinewy fluid undulating – fully expanding my energy*
> *– touching the outer rim of the universe*
> **Yes! Right There...**
> *what joy*
> *exciting – bursting – blowing up from the inside out*
> *– loving it with every pore, nerve, of me*
> **Yes! Right There...**
> *what ecstasy*
> *the inner core – hot, boiling – expanding universal boundaries*
> *– it feels so damn good*
> **Yes! Right There...**
> *Complete fulfillment – satisfaction – total bliss, living the joy,*
> *experiencing exquisite ecstasy*
> **Yes! Right There, Yes! Right There**
> **Yes! Right There...**
>
> *Denise L. Cook, The Oracle*

58. Occasionally, Give Without Being Asked expecting nothing in return. As Kahlil Gibran says in *The Prophet*, "It is well to give when asked, but it is better to give unasked through understanding." So offer to do something special for your lover without having them feel the need to return the gesture. Just make the lovemaking all about them sometimes and not about yourself. During some of your lovemaking sessions, pleasure your lover with a surprise—soft music, candlelight, "honey dusting," a full body massage, a complete body kissing or licking, topped-off with edible panties or underwear; or maybe even an oral sex treat with chocolate, ice or an added whipped cream delight. Just trust us, your mate will be in heaven! Even the Bible agrees… asserting, "It's better to give than receive."

Don't always expect immediate returns on your investment in good unselfish lovemaking. Like a good stock, it will appreciate over time and pay good dividends. And take note—The grass is always greener… if you water it!

59. Learn How To Give and Receive Oral Sex. In *The Big Black Book*, it says that, "Oral sex is practiced by more than 85% of women questioned by *Cosmopolitan* and 95% of those by *Playboy*." And data from a 2002 U.S. Department of Health and Human Services survey states that 90% of men and women between the ages of 25-44 have had oral sex.

Oral sex is a delicacy that's always in season. Like *Lawry's Seasoned Salt*, it goes with everything. For example, it comes in handy if people aren't quite ready to have intercourse; it can suffice if one can't have sex due to illness or injury; it can relieve couples who want to avoid pregnancy; it can resurrect and save lovemaking sessions gone badly; and, because it feels so wonderful, it can make a marginal sexual experience fantastic.

Moreover, the great thing about oral sex is that it's a dish that can be served during any phase of your sexual meal. It can be enjoyed as an appetizer before intercourse, the main course, itself, or as an after intercourse cocktail.

Although, as pleasurable as it may be to most who engage in it, some people, because of religious, cultural and/or societal abhorrence, still have inhibitions or "hang-ups" concerning oral sex. This makes it difficult for them to enjoy giving it or receiving pleasure from it. Some may think that they are not good at it, while others are simply self-conscious and worry about the smell, taste, or look of their genitals and the highly intimate nature of the sexual act, itself. However, in *The Complete Idiot's Guide to Amazing Sex*, Sari Locker notes, "... There is no reason to worry that your genitals smell or taste bad if you've kept up with basic hygiene. Your genitals have a distinct taste and smell, but that's your natural aroma. It's part of *you*. The same goes for the way your genitals look, or how much pubic hair you have, or even how long it takes you to have an orgasm. Don't worry that oral sex is uncomfortable or 'gross' to the person who's having oral sex with you. It's not! It is an amazing part of sex."

In The *Redbook* Report on Female Sexuality, it says that up to 80 percent of the 100,000 women they surveyed found that oral sex was enjoyable and that only 6 percent found it "unpleasant" or "taboo." Although the percentages of women in other surveys have shown oral sex not to be quite as gratifying as the Redbook Report, they all seem to indicate that the majority of women found it more enjoyable than not. Nevertheless, you should not have oral sex because of what other men and women have said in surveys, but because it's something that works for you and your partner; not because you feel you *have to*, but because you *want to*.

About Fellatio: If you've decided to engage in oral sex and you're performing oral sex on your male partner, (technically called fellatio), there are a few things to think about. Try to avoid having your teeth touch his penis and never bite it. *The Complete Idiot's Guide to Amazing Sex* says before he ejaculates you must decide whether to remove your mouth from his penis and let him ejaculate on himself, somewhere on you, the bed or into a cloth or towel. You may also opt to have him ejaculate in your mouth and then discreetly discharge it into a tissue; or, just swallow his semen.

Most men prefer that their partners swallow, because it most resembles the effect of having an orgasm during intercourse. Also, some men report that during oral sex the orgasm seems much more intense when they have mouth-to-penis contact. Nonetheless, if there are any questions about how it should be handled, then discuss it with your partner ahead of time; that way you'll know exactly what to do and avoid awkwardly interrupting the pleasure that oral sex is meant to provide.

For the curious women who may be concerned about what comprises his velvety liquid juice, *The Complete Idiot's Guide to Amazing Sex*, states that, "Semen contains proteins, vitamins and sugars, and between 10 and 40 calories per ejaculation. Some people hate the taste, others find it erotic."

About Cunnilingus: If you've decided to engage in oral sex, and you're performing oral sex on your female partner, there are a few things you need to be aware of and take into account. With oral sex, much as with life, women tend to be multifaceted and a bit more complex than men. While pleasuring men orally is a more 'one size fits all', to the contrary, women are very multidimensional and more suited for 'different strokes for different folks.'

Sari Locker says, "Performing oral sex on a woman, called *cunnilingus*, is a great way to pleasure a woman and to experience her sensuality. Through oral sex, her partner can see, smell, taste, and closely stimulate her. Her partner can experience her orgasm in a way that is different from intercourse—up close and personal. In fact, some women can have orgasms more easily from oral sex than from intercourse because they're getting the direct stimulation to their clitoris. Whether it makes a woman have an orgasm more easily or not, many women love the feeling of oral sex simply because of the unique sensation of a warm, wet tongue on their vulva."

What's important to remember is that each woman may like something totally different and in many cases exactly the opposite of other women. Some women say they are excited to have a slow rhythmic pace with the tongue softly, just barely touching the clitoris; while others said they prefer to have it quick paced and hard with a firm suck of the clitoris. Yet again, some women say they liked to have their nipples kissed, breast fondled and maybe a finger inserted into their vagina during oral sex. Whereas some women didn't like their breast being touched at all and instead favored having their buttocks squeezed and their anal area stimulated, and maybe a lubricated finger inserted into their anus. Some preferred all of the above. So, a word to the wise, make absolutely no assumptions about women regarding oral sex!

Oral sex can certainly be a sexual thrill ride for most couples, yet both participants must be ready, willing, and most of all, comfortable with each other in order to receive the maximum joy and pleasure from it.

So guys, in most cases, 'If you learn how to lick it, the more she'll let you stick it', and, 'If you know how to lick-her, she'll come quicker'.

Just a note: Be sure to get an understanding with your mate as to what constitutes cheating, because like Bill Clinton might say, "Eatin' ain't Cheatin'."

As with any intimate sexual contact, safety should be your first consideration. HIV (the virus that causes AIDS) and other STD's (sexually transmitted diseases) can be contracted when having sex orally.

New Diet

*Honey, I've found a New Diet,
but you have to help me stay on it...
It's a healthy, all natural, non-fat, lo-cal, no carb diet.
What I like most about it is—there are no restrictions...
you can partake anytime, as much as you like,
morning, noon or night—whenever you're up for it!
Unlike other diets, it's recommended and often works
better late night before bed and
seems really effective first thing in the morning.
Like Folger's, it's "The best part of waking up..."
Like Lite beer from Miller, it
"Tastes Great" and is "Less Filling."
Like M&M's, it "...Melts in your mouth not in your hands"
Like Campbell's Soup, it's "M'm! M'm! Good!"
Like a Timex, "It takes a licking and keeps on ticking,"
Like Almond Joy, "Sometimes you feel like a nut..."
Like Maxwell House, it's "Good to the last drop!" and
Like McDonald's, "I'm lovin' it!"
However, there is one side effect, it's a-dick-ting...*

Julie Lovelace

60. **You Can't Lose With the Stuff I Use.** Ladies, after having brought him to ejaculation, if you really want to send him through the roof—immediately place his penis in your mouth and perform oral sex. If you do that and swallow, you'll *always* keep him "coming" back for more.

Wake Up Call

*Lying in my bed
in the wee hours of the morning
I feel something
soft, warm, and wet between my legs.
Waking slightly,
I recognize the feather-soft lapping
of your tongue exploring my pussy.
Pretending to be asleep,
I shift slightly
to give you a better angle.
Don't want you to
struggle getting at what
I'm so willing to give.
Peeking through sleep soaked eyes
I watch you eating my breakfast.
Savoring the sight
of satisfaction creeping up
on both of us.
Fully awake now and fully involved
in this luscious wake-up call.
Spasms of happiness
Ripple from my navel to my toes
As you raise your head
Just enough to look at me and say,
"Good morning, baby."*

Saphron

Chinese proverb says, "Foolish man give wife grand piano, wise man give wife upright organ."

61. **One Good Turn Deserves Another.** Guys, if you are fortunate enough to bring your lover to orgasm with your penis vaginally, immediately after, perform oral sex on her; if you do it right, you'll always keep her "coming" back for more—provided you continue to treat her right in all the other important aspects of your relationship!

Love's Harvest

*If you fail to **Plant** the **Seeds** of
Sincere Unconditional Love, Mutual Respect,
Good Communication, Understanding,
Honesty & Trust in the
Springtime of your relationship…
Don't expect to **Harvest**
Mouth-watering, Sweet, Juicy, Delicious, Tasty,
Succulent, Long Lasting, Flavor Filled Love in the **Fall**.*

Julie Lovelace

---

62. **Don't Be Afraid To Lose Control and Let Go.** Some of you, and maybe even most of you, have probably never truly experienced the most that an orgasm has to offer. For those of you who orgasm regularly you know what a wonderful feeling having an orgasm is. According to a 1994 *Sex in America* survey conducted by the University of Chicago, researchers noted that three-fourths of men reach orgasm while having sexual intercourse, but less than one-third of women did from coitus.

However, don't rush to get the tissue and start feeling sorry for women—because when they do orgasm, they have a much easier time experiencing multiple orgasms and can maintain a feeling of sexual arousal much longer then men. One clinical study by the sex experts William H. Masters, M.D., and Virginia E. Johnson, of the former

Masters and Johnson Institute in St. Louis, reported that in a laboratory setting a woman can go on to experience wave after orgasmic wave—as many as 134. Men tend to cool down right away. And depending on age, desire and many other arousal factors, it may take men minutes or even days to become hot and hard again.

I mentioned all that to say that orgasms are not always as easily attainable as we would like them to be. So we need to make the most out of the orgasms we do have. Yet, rarely do we allow ourselves to drink the whole cup of ecstasy that an orgasm can produce. We just won't "let go." When we're just about to have it all and experience the sexual "Big Bang," we try to move away with an intense sense of fear that comes over us making us feel like we can't handle it. Well you can handle it! You just have to get over the fear of losing control and be *willing* to just totally "lose it." You may have a better chance when you're having sex with someone you feel comfortable enough and trust to: bite, kick, punch and talk nasty and dirty to. You may also want to be in a place where you feel safe and secure enough to scream, holler, swear, yell, etc. Don't expect to have this experience all the time, but when you feel it coming on, you better go for it! It may be the closest thing to heaven you'll experience while still here on earth. As the Chinese proverb confirms, "Panties *not* best thing on earth, but *next* to best thing on earth!"

If for any reason you are having difficulty participating in sexual activities or feel sexually unfulfilled, we recommend that you contact a qualified, licensed, professional sex, marriage or family therapist that has experience relating to your particular situation or circumstance. You may be surprised to learn that in most cases help can be provided.

As We

As we lay together today,
You touched my spirit
And my soul rose only god knows how high
As we lay together today,
Shockwaves permeated my very flesh

Like exploding atoms I must confess
As we lay in each others arms
Holding firm, holding tight, holding…still
I melted and we became one
Pressing my body firmly into yours
I feel the expanse of your manhood
Your hand pressed firmly into that space
that defines both form and structure
The other firmly cupping what so obviously fits,
belongs to you…you
You grow, attached yet set alone, locked in this deep,
sweet, tight, wet abyss
Your essence is burning inside me, nurtures me,
is a part of my being like DNA
Twisting and spiraling in infinity, we fit like hand in glove,
skin in skin, heart in heart
Synergy, fire, electricity, earth quaking,
connecting the dots from joy, to passion,
To exquisite ecstasy.
You bring me to a point of ecstasy never before realized
Where you begin I end,
where I begin you already were, are,
we are one…
As we lay together as one today,
I realized what perfect love is,
I realized what perfect being is,
I realized I was in heaven
As we lay together today,
You touched my spirit
And my heart rose to meet yours
Yes, we were one and in HEAVEN
As we lay together today

Denise L. Cook, The Oracle

Things to Say or Do During Sex

"When being showered with love, clothing is optional…"

"Men: Don't forget, after making love—women love to cuddle…"

Chapter Five

Things to Say or Do After Sex

Now that you may have had an orgasm or two, doesn't mean the lovemaking is over, quite the contrary—it's just beginning. The last time you had sex isn't over until you're having sex again. So, keep this in mind and commit it to memory and practice. 'Great sex never ends until it begins again, and foreplay is all day'.

> **If You Cum In Love...**
>
> *If you "cum" in love, you shall go in peace...*
>
> *R. Ray Barnes*

63. Keep It Real. Find something about your lover that you can genuinely compliment her or him on, before, during and after you make love. Flattery does work, if it's sincere; lying doesn't. If your mate is not the greatest looker, don't suggest otherwise. However, if you sincerely feel that your mate is beautiful or handsome, then look him or her in the eye and say so. However, don't exaggerate or placate your lover. No matter how cunning and slick you may think you are, people know when you're being sincere and when you're just trying to bulls#*%—especially women. They don't call it "a woman's intuition" for nothing.

When making love, relax. It doesn't have to be command performances every time; just try to make it exciting and interesting. Eye contact, sensuous touching, and heartfelt compliments always help.

64. Men, If You Snooze You Lose. Don't forget the "afterplay." This is when foreplay truly begins. However, whatever you do, don't make the mistake of going to sleep immediately after you have sex or make love to her. You must learn to *appreciate* that most women like to cuddle after they make love—and they never forget the men who love to cuddle with them—and they forever hold it against the ones who don't!

Sex and Relationship Therapist, Ian Kerner, Ph.D., author of *She Comes First* and *Be Honest—You're Not That In To Him Either*, says there's a reason females love to cuddle. In August of 2005, on an episode of *Strictly Sex With Dr. Drew*, he said, "There are many hormones that are released during sex and that in women one of those hormones is Oxytocin, which plays a role in labor, breast feeding and bonding, and is often dubbed the 'cuddle hormone' and is heavily released during sex and orgasm. Studies have shown that if women after sex have nothing there to cuddle with on an emotional level, that sometimes the Oxytocin does the opposite, it triggers a sense of sadness."

So men, after sex you mustn't forget to cuddle. Women are passionate, sensitive, caring and very emotional. They want to be reassured that after they've just given you the most precious thing they have, (their bodies, and in some cases their mind), that when you're finished, you don't simply get up, walk away and toss them aside.

So the absolute worst thing you can do is leave immediately after you have sex. You should let her know what your intentions are and how long you plan to stay before you come over to have sex; in this way she can decide whether your "booty call" is acceptable to her. Never make a lady feel the *only* reason you "came" to see her was just for the sex. Believe it or not, she has a whole lot more to offer than what is between her legs! And hopefully you have a lot more to give than what's between yours.

> ### *Stop, Look and Listen*
>
> **I Stopped Listening**
> *to the sensuously pleasing sound of your voice—*
> and **Started Listening**
> *to the sweet angelic inner-sound of your* **SOUL**...
> **I Stopped Admiring**
> *the awesome child-like beauty of your smile—*
> and **Started Admiring**
> *the remarkable inner-beauty of your* **MIND**...
> **I Stopped Measuring**
> *the cute little perky size of your breast—*
> and **Started Measuring**
> *the enormously huge inner-size of your* **HEART**...
> **I Stopped Looking**
> *at the sexy curvaceous shape of your body—*
> and **Started Looking**
> *at the well rounded inner-shape of your* **SPIRIT**...
> *And now,*
> **I truly see YOU—**
> *completely* **naked** *and* **unabashed**...
> *and mere words are not enough to convey
> how really* **WONDERFUL** *I think you are...*
>
> *R. Ray Barnes*

65. **Guys, Shut Up!** Even though it's quite common for you to brag to your close friends about most anything you do that turns out successful (especially those few occasions when you demonstrate sexual prowess), it's a good idea to keep intimate sexual details with a woman that you love and care about to an absolute minimum; women will appreciate that. If for some reason you'd like to boast about some sexual encounter you had at the Mustang Ranch (one of the world's most infamous brothels), that's one thing, but don't do it in regards to that special someone that you have, or intend to have, a serious loving relationship with. Actually, you shouldn't spread private intimate information about any true "lady," whether you intend a serious relationship or not, because if she respected you enough to allow you to sleep with her, then you should respect her enough to keep the details to yourself. If you have any comments you'd like to make about the sexual experience you had with her, then tell her, not your friends.

However, with men it can be quite the opposite. **Ladies, Speak Up!** If you feel that you are close enough, a carefully worded general comment about how good he was sexually to one of his best or trusted friends, who you are sure will tell him, will do wonders in feeding his

"All I need is you..."

ego. For men, hearing great news like that from a best friend is like having their egos treated to dinner at Masa in New York or the French Laundry in Napa Valley, California.

Contrary to popular belief, men are more sensitive than women in certain areas, sexual performance being at the top of the list. Most women can perform sexually with just a desire to do so, though for men it can be much more psychologically challenging. In most cases, great sex is determined by how well the man performs. It's up to him to get it up, keep it up and not ejaculate prematurely. If he's successful up to that point, he must still proceed at the right pace, not too fast, but not too slow, either. He must thrust, not too hard, yet not too soft. Though we could go on and on, I think you see my point. Men probably secretly worry more about how they perform sexually than anything else.

Entwined In Love

After making love—
We lay here with
Our Legs
XXX Crossed XXX
inside of each other's inside…
Our arms—
Once stiff and outstretched,
Now seem
Double jointed, twisted and distorted…
Your naturally curly hair—
Now looks like dreads all locked together,
Just like our bodies were an orgasm ago…
Your life crisscrossed with my life—
Your mind-melted in-2-my-mind
As our hearts and our souls lay
Entwined in love…

R. Ray Barnes

But keep in mind, ladies, although hearing from his friend that his performance was admirable validates what he's been secretly boasting and simultaneously launches his ego into the stratosphere, it's still always best to tell him directly how you felt about the lovemaking.

66. Don't Expect Your Lover To Love You the Way You Would Love You; and don't expect your lover to think like you or respond like you to the same stimulus. In other words, don't expect a dog to behave like a cat; he will fail every time. You must measure a dog's behavior on a dog scale. Your lover may be giving you what you want, but you may be measuring it on the wrong scale. Michelle McKinney Hammond says, in her book, *Sassy, Single, & Satisfied,* "Women struggle with men because they want men to be like them. They are not. The struggle would end if we could learn to see our differences as challenges to our own personalities."

You must accept your lover for who *that person is*, not who you imagine him or her to be after you change them. Author, Don Miguel Ruiz says in his inspiring book based on Toltec wisdom, *The Four Agreements,* "We don't need to justify love; it is there or not there. Real love is accepting other people the way they are without trying to change them. If we try to change them, this means we don't really like them."

More so, we must recognize their *capability* and *capacity* to love. If their overall capability and capacity to love is acceptable to you, rather than complaining or trying to change them, help them to reach their full potential. If it's unacceptable, then maybe you should seek a more suitable lover. Because you *must* understand, "A gallon can only hold a gallon, no matter how much you try to pour into it."

And regardless of how much one may shower you with loving accolades, unless their praise and adoration manifests itself in their behavior toward you, take it with a grain of salt. When someone truly cares about you, loves you and adores you, it should be evident by the way they treat you. As stated in Matthew, Chapter 7: Verse 20 of *The Living Bible,* Jesus The Christ, said, "Yes, the way to identify a tree or a person is by the kind of fruit produced."

67. **Measuring A Man's Love Is** quite **Different Than** measuring **A Woman's Love.** I've learned from Dr. Phil that women express their emotions openly and verbally, while men disguise theirs in all sorts of weird behaviors that women must learn to decipher to truly understand how he feels about her. You can't always trust what a man says, not because he's lying, but because men will run from questions of intimacy, love or what they perceive as control as if they were running from the plague or Lorena Bobbitt. Consequently, a man will often say whatever he thinks a woman wants to hear just to keep from having to talk further about it—or he will tend to be very evasive. Yogi Bhajan says, "When a man speaks, usually he begins by talking around the subject, rarely beginning with the real subject at hand. For instance, when a woman asks her husband what time he will return, he will say: 'After work'. She wants to know what time he will be home. He will answer, 'About five or five-thirty'. Men are often unwilling to commit to a specific answer, time or place, as it appears in their minds to limit or weaken their power."

As a consequence, ladies may want to pay closer attention to what he does as opposed to what he says. Again, Dr. Phil says men frequently express their emotions and love through things they value. Find out what he likes, loves, treasures and *really* cares about and how you measure up to those things. If he values his time and he shares a lot of it with you, that may indicate more about how he feels than anything he says. Apply that principle to other things he may love: car, home, money, kids, etc., and evaluate how much of those things he has been sharing with you. This in no way means that you should disregard everything he *says* about love and intimacy; it's just another way for you to *hear* what he's not saying.

Some of the ideas expressed in #66 and #67 were taken from a June 2003 issue of O, *The Oprah Magazine,* in an article, "Dr. Phil's MANual," written by Phillip C. McGraw, PhD, best selling author and nationally syndicated TV talk show host affectionately known as Dr. Phil.

Do I Ever Cross Your Mind?

And she questioned him saying,
"Do I ever cross your mind when we're not together?"
And in silence, to himself, he said...

I THINK OF YOU
when dawn draws near...
as the sun oozes out of the sea,
creeping across the sky chasing darkness away...
'I' Think Of You

I HEAR YOUR VOICE
when the birds sing...
whistling their morning anthems of love,
chirping sweet melodies
manifesting the beauty of sound...
'I' Hear Your Voice

I FEEL YOUR TOUCH
when the dew falls...
touching and kissing softly the flowers,
weeping tears of joy on the leaves of trees,
and licking *me* all over...
'I' Feel Your Touch

I SEE YOUR FACE
when dusk closes in...
as the moon works the nightshift,
shining it's spotlight on the stars
who all won academy awards for best picture...
'I' See Your Face
...but as she looked on anxiously awaiting his answer,
in a very nonchalant way, he replied...
'Yeah, Sometimes...'

R. Ray Barnes

68. Being Turned On and Turned Off Sexually. Even though there are things about a person that may turn you on sexually, it doesn't necessarily mean that the person will be a good lover or good in bed. While a person may have a super hot body, be a great looker, have a sexy walk, be a sensual dancer, freaky and uninhibited when talking about sex, this doesn't always mean your man will be sexually satisfying. Consequently, don't expect too much from any first time sexual encounter; so don't relinquish the quest right away. If you still find yourself sexually attracted to that person, give it some time for both of you to develop a level of comfort and sexual expression; a sexual charisma. It may take a few lovemaking sessions before you feel a sexual chemistry. Even though someone who turns you on may not result in great sex the first time, being turned on is half the battle. It helps to create desire, and desire is a very important element in having great sex. So, having a partner who has the ability to excite you sexually is definitely a plus.

However, being excited and turned-on sexually may mean something totally different to each individual. This subject is classic for illustrating the proverbial statement, "Different strokes for different folks" and "One man's trash may be another man's treasure." So to assist you with a few things that you may do to turn your lover on and to help you add some spicy flavor to your romantic dish, we've listed some ideas and sexy traits that may be a turn-on for some. As we have stated earlier, turning your lover on and having great sex is more mental than physical. The collective actions that affectionately touch the heart and mind of your lover is often more of a turn-on than merely saying or doing something sexual or physical. All you need to realize is that, "As one thinks on the inside, shall be reflected on the outside." Or, "Wherever the mind goes, the ass will follow."

And, as a general rule, be willing to have sex anytime and anywhere it's safe to do so. Avoid having predetermined restrictions such as: I've just gotten my hair done—I don't want to wrinkle my dress—not now, the game is on—I'm trying to sleep right now—not in the kitchen—not on the floor, etc.—remember, spontaneity is a sexual turn-on.

Examine the list and see if you feel comfortable using any of these ideas to turn your lover on.

"Forecast: Hot and humid with a chance of love showers…"

Forty Ways To Turn Your Lover On

+ Present flowers to your lover and sometimes surprise him or her with thoughtful gifts—don't just wait for Valentine's Day, Birthdays, etc. To add to the surprise, wrap your gifts!

+ Be unique. Occasionally be creative and personalize your gifts. Amaze your lover with something that you've designed, created or made especially for him or her.

+ Surprise your lover with tickets to a play, concert or something that you know he or she would really enjoy.

+ Write, give and/or read love poems to your lover.

+ Create a sexy pet name for your lover and use it.

+ Say "yes," "please," "thank you," "honey," "darling," "sweetheart," "sugar," "baby" & "I love you" more often… and any other phrases or sayings that you like that express affection.

+ Make it customary to compliment your lover. Be kind, gracious, appreciative, and show gratitude.

+ Show your lover how important he or she is and how much you care about your lover by canceling, delaying, or postponing that really special meeting or whatever you have to do, just so you could spend some more time with this one special person.

+ For no special reason, occasion or time, tell your lover how much you truly appreciate him or her being in your life.

+ Always try to be open and honest about your feelings and unafraid to express what your lover means to you.

+ Remember, foreplay is all day. Send sexy and flirtatious voice, text and e-mail messages throughout the day.

+ Be enticing with your lover. Playfully tease, touch, whisper and smile at him or her and make erotic gestures.

- *Be playful, loosen up and have fun. Dance, play sports, cards and games with your lover. Have pillow fights, wrestle, tickle each other, laugh out loud and just be silly once in a while.*
- *Never miss a chance to kiss and hug your lover. Display and practice random acts of love, kindness and affection.*
- *Take turns making your lover King or Queen for a day—then do whatever your partner says for 24 hours.*
- *Go for walks on the beach under the moonlight and walk hand-in-hand in the park with your lover.*
- *Watch a sunset or a sunrise together.*
- *Go on planned and unplanned picnics.*
- *Prepare and serve breakfast in bed to your lover—even if you're not such a great cook. It's the thought and effort that really counts.*
- *Take unplanned intimate weekend pleasure trips.*
- *Fireplaces and hot tubs are wonderful aphrodisiacs, use them more often to inspire and enhance your lovemaking.*
- *Plan a trip to an erotic hotel. (Just Google "erotic hotels.")*
- *Sometimes have impromptu hot and sweaty sex. And make love outdoors or somewhere you know you shouldn't.*
- *When you're alone with your lover, dress for your sexual success. If you've got it flaunt it! Wear outfits that highlight your most sexy features—be tempting and have fun doing it!*
- *When you're feeling real sexy, sometimes just walk around nude. Sleep in the nude sometimes and hold each other through the night.*
- *While lying in bed listening to the rain, lovingly embrace your lover and whisper how wonderful and sexy she or he is.*
- *Make it an interesting project and try making love in every room of your house. If you have a pool or spa skynny-dip together.*

- ✦ Make the mood sexy by lighting scented candles and placing them around the bedroom and bath areas or even throughout the house.
- ✦ Make loving each other special. Dance and celebrate a night of love and passion with a toast of wine or Champagne.
- ✦ Spend some time just lying in bed looking at and holding each other, and the first one who talks loses. You decide on the prize for the winner—but make it a sexual treat.
- ✦ Feed your lover delicious treats in bed or just make her or him the treat by adding whipped cream or edible underwear.
- ✦ In your most sexy voice, read erotic poetry to your lover before making love.
- ✦ Give your lover a bath followed by a full body massage using scented oils, strategic kisses and sensual whispers.
- ✦ While making love, look passionately into the eyes of your partner; and after you both climax, embrace your lover and sincerely say that your lover is beautiful or handsome and say, "I love you."
- ✦ Exercise your fantasies. Dress-up, role-play and perform a sexy strip tease—shining a flashlight for the spotlight.
- ✦ It's okay to be naughty sometimes. Occasionally use sex toys, talk dirty and watch erotic videos during lovemaking.
- ✦ When pleasing your lover do it with enthusiasm! Make her or him feel like there's nothing else you'd rather be doing.
- ✦ Be spontaneous—ravish your lover as soon as he or she comes through the door. Don't always plan your lovemaking; just let it happen—anytime, any place…and don't resist.
- ✦ Fresh out of the shower, while still wet, throw your lover on the bed, perform oral sex and then make love to him/her.
- ✦ When away from home, have phone sex with your lover.

✦ ✦ ✦

Being sexually *turned-off* has to be given just as much consideration as being turned-on. While the mental ramifications may be the same for men and women, the physical ramifications are quite different. There is nothing worse for a man than to be turned-off, after having become sexually aroused just prior to having sex. So ladies, if want your lover to make passionate love to you, then you should tread lightly and be very careful about the negative or unflattering things you say at this juncture. Don't let the macho exteriors fool you. Men are very sensitive and the wrong comment at a time like this can make a *hard* guy go very soft. Often times when he goes down, he may be out for the count—and getting him to stand erect again may take more than a notion, an emotion, erotic lotion or a voodoo love potion. So try to maintain an overall positive attitude and outlook regarding anything you say or do. This is not the time to bring up past indiscretions or to complain about something. If you've chosen to get to this point, anything negative can wait. And guys, she, too, may be very sensitive at this time; so it's wise for you to be cognizant of what you say to her, too. This is a time for loving, not fighting. As Chinese proverb says, "Man who fight with wife all day, get no *piece* at night."

Also, be sure to check your body odor, breath, and the general cleanliness of your private parts. Try to make no comments unless they're complimentary. If you're having a problem with something in particular about your lover, rather than complaining about it do something positive and proactive to encourage correction.

69. **What's Love Got To Do With It?** The power of uniting in love is one of the most powerful forces in the universe. When you inner-connect spiritually with that special someone, that special "true love," your "soul mate," the energy created from this spiritual union of love gives birth to a oneness that transforms you and your mate into a single, more dynamic source for love and manifestation of love; much greater than either of you could be alone, whose capacity *for* and capability *to* love increases exponentially. When this occurs, by virtue of the power and impact inherent in such a fusion of love, it will become the most important occurrence in your life—and could very well be the closest thing you'll *ever* experience that mirrors and reflects the "first love" that the creator had for human kind.

Don't expect the same feelings and sensations to occur when making love with someone you're *in* love with compared to someone with whom you're not *in* love with. It's really an unfair comparison. When all other factors are equal, love adds a dimension to sex and lovemaking that is impossible to match.

For most women and for some men, sex without all of the emotion, intimacy and passion of being in love is interesting for a while, but it wears out over long periods of time. If the act of "lovemaking" doesn't ultimately lead to "making love," then one might ask, "What good is it?" It can be likened to filling the car with gas, starting it up, yet, never leaving the driveway. But, when it comes to describing the difference between having sex and making love, I think Colette Williams, mother of two says it best, "For me sex is a physical act that takes, and making love is a spiritual act that gives."

Although it is true that, "Love *is* what love does," we must be aware of our own actions and how these may affect the manner in which people *love us*. This notion is aptly epitomized in the following quote by Robert Murray, an extraordinary painter, artist and Art Instructor at Concordia University in Montreal, Canada: "If you plant corn in me you will get back corn, not wheat, but corn!" Keeping that in mind, we must be very careful to *sow* seeds of *love* if we expect to *reap* the sweet fruits of *love*.

So, in spite of what Tina Turner voiced in her Grammy Award winning song, *What's Love Got To Do With It?* You should know that love's got *everything* to do with it! But if you're still finding yourself asking that question, then maybe you should try it sometime. Because when love's in the house, the house is truly a home.

In addition, never give up on finding your one true love–it's there for you... So use your past relationships as dress rehearsals for your new relationship until you reach your command performance. And last but not least, one very important thing to remember: don't assume that anything regarding a love relationship is "so clear that it goes without saying." When it comes to love, leave no room for misunderstanding—take the time to make it clear by saying it!

Lastly, remember, Dr. Phil says that marriages and love relationships are not 50-50, but each partner must contribute 100-100!

Love Is Never Having To Say...

*You wash my troubles away,
you bathe my thoughts, and you massage my heart
with passionate emotions of love...*
**So You Don't Have To Say You Love Me,
Because I Already Know.**
*You're always there when i need you,
if not in person, in spirit,
i can feel your love, concern and affection.*
**So You Don't Have To Say You Love Me,
Because I Already Know.**
*In dark rooms on pillows of love,
when our bodies become a physical eclipse and
our hearts become our vision, we always see eye to eye...*
**So You Don't Have To Say You Love Me,
Because I Already Know.**
*When sorrow beckons me,
you mystically appear with expressions of joyfulness
and my sorrow vanishes like a desert mirage...*
**So You Don't Have To Say You Love Me,
Because I Already Know.**
*True **Love** is **Never Having To Say**, "I Love You."
...but, then again, i sure **Love** it when you do!*

R. Ray Barnes

Things to Say or Do After Sex

"I've got your number—360-100-24-7-365…"

"It's a Love Dream…"

Afterword

If you were to try any of the advice, suggestions and principals expressed in this book, I guarantee it will enhance your sex life and love relationships for a short time. But if you truly desire to become better at sex and love consistently, it will take more—you have to work at it. That means you can't just apply these principals when it's convenient or fifteen minutes before you want to make love. You must make sex, love and relationship building a routine and complete part of your life. Best-selling author and radio personality Dr. Dean Edell agrees that it takes a dedicated effort to improve your sex life, "People invest years in improving their golf swing but cannot see the logic dictating that something as intricate as sex can take two people lots of practice to explore and perfect."

If anything, after having read *69 Ways To Better Relationships, Sex and Love*, one should have learned, at the very least, that a successful

---

Love...

*Love... there is nothing else like love—
and else you have love you have nothing...*

R. Ray Barnes

marriage, having good sex, and a wonderful relationship are all works in progress. In most marriages and committed relationships, couples often express how they feel about one another when they're angry or upset—not when their spirits are high and happy. We must learn to work through our anger and not allow our anger to work through us. So make an effort to share the positive things about your relationship with your mate when you're feeling good. And, if you ever feel trapped inside your anger, remember what Eckhart Tolle stated in his extraordinary work, *The Power of Now (A Guide To Spiritual Enlightenment)*, "When there's no way out, there's still always a way through."

One secret to keeping your love upbeat and joyful is to never stop "dating" your mate after you get married or enter into a committed relationship. Don't get so comfortable and complacent that you lose the enthusiasm and passion for your lover. Women, on occasion, you should dress up and "look cute" for him like you did when you were trying to attract his attention. And men, don't become couch potatoes now that you've captured her; still ask her out once in a while, the way you used to when you were trying to keep her interest.

Don't stop fixing your hair, dressing nicely, wearing perfume and cologne and complimenting each other. If you continue that *dating* attitude, you can keep your relationship fresh, exciting, active and fun. Remember, the same things you did to get your mate are exactly the same things you need to do to keep your mate!

Don't *sweat* the small stuff, but acknowledge it and pay close attention to its effects. Small things left unchecked often grow into big things that can be cancerous to a loving relationship. It's somewhat similar to our body weight when left unchecked it can lead to a heart attack. Similarly, in relationships, small things, left unchecked, can lead to heartbreak.

Find ways of accentuating the beautiful and positive aspects in your relationship, while working on eliminating the unattractive and negative things—this also includes positive and negative people. Our relationships are like flower gardens; although beautiful and inspiring, from time to time we must rid the garden of unsightly weeds or they will eventually overtake the flowers and destroy the beauty of the garden.

And when discussing relationship issues, do so without blaming each other. In your conversations try to identify the strengths and weaknesses of your relationship. Look closely at the things you love about it that work well, as well as the things you may not be so happy with that need improvement.

Once you've identified the strengths and weaknesses of your relationship, use effective communication to resolve the issues; again, without blaming one another. Relationship goals are often very personal and differences in opinion can cause disharmony. Often, lovers discover they are quite dissimilar. One mate may be conservative, a saver, and need to take things slow before acting. The other may be impulsive, an eager 'let's-dive-right-in' type. It's important to keep the lines of communication open in order to form a compromise that suits the both of you and that each of you can feel good about.

As a way to help you accomplish this, share with your lover three things you love about your relationship, three things you love about them, three things you love that your mate does *to* you and three things you'd like for your mate to do more often. When you're done with your list, have fun exploring what you've discovered about each other—then watch the magic happen.

Relationships Take Hard Work, Dedication and Commitment

Any one of you can luck-up a time or two and hit a three-point basketball shot, make three strikes in a row in bowling or hit a homerun in baseball. However, if you want to become a great basketball player, bowler or baseball player, we all know it will take a burning desire, hard work, dedication, practice and a certain amount of commitment and skill; and to become a great lover, mate, husband or wife will take all of those things and even more. So let's face it, all of you won't become great lovers, but all of you who follow the advice and principals set forth here can certainly become better lovers, mates, husbands and wives.

Yogi Bhajan says, "The feeling of 'being in love' is fulfilling and enticing. However, people can be addicted to this experience. They search for one relationship after another, to get the rush of 'being in love'. They never move into the more mature stages of love.... When a man and a woman are truly merged in a relationship, a new element emerges. The goal is to become two bodies and one soul." When you are able to become one with your lover, that great addicting feeling of being in love is even more intensified.

To achieve the "one soul" objective in your relationship as Yogi Bhajan speaks of and to discover the kind of lover you will become depends greatly on the level of trust, care, concern, commitment, understanding and degree of vulnerability you are willing to exhibit towards your mate. You can only experience love and pleasure equal to the amount of your vulnerability. Not until you allow yourself to take the risk to be vulnerable, will you ever truly experience all the pleasure of what love and sex were meant to be. You must learn to let yourself go and free yourself from the fear of falling in love and not being caught by your lover. It's called truly *trusting* one another. Trusting, in the same way that a baby fearlessly entrusts the father who tosses him or her high up in the air, just laughing freely, knowing that he or she will be caught.

Imagine yourself just "free falling" in love, trusting all along the way that your lover will catch you. If you can do that, you have the potential of experiencing the greatest love you've ever known.

Free Falling...

***You've* got *Me* high, so high**
in the stratosphere of my emotions,
that now i feel myself
Falling, Falling...
Free Falling in Love with you.
i've kicked caution to the wind,
as my journey towards love begins,
drifting through soft clouds of joy,
with no abort switch to deploy,
as i feel myself

> ***Falling, Falling...***
> ***Free Falling** in **Love** with **you.***
> *i have no parachute in my gear,*
> *no safety net to ease my fear,*
> *no ocean waters to break my fall,*
> *and no emergency personnel to call,*
> *i'm just*
> ***Falling, Falling...***
> ***Free Falling** in **Love** with **you.***
> *i'm falling so fancy free,*
> *with my faith in our love to be,*
> *aided by a gentle breeze of ecstasy,*
> *with only your heart i entrust to catch me,*
> *as i am in deed*
> ***Falling, Falling...***
> ***Free Falling** in **Love** with **you.***
>
> *Julie Lovelace*

Another important key to loving, making love and having great sex is the ability to "like" someone. Someone you like is someone you can enjoy doing 'nothing' with. Loving someone is not difficult. We love many of our relatives; however, we may not really *like* them. To love someone is a beautiful thing and is rather easy to do, but to like someone can be hard as hell! In order for men and women to truly be *in* love with one another, they must first truly *like* one another. For example, men of course enjoy women sexually; that's easy. Yet for a man to truly be *in* love with a woman he needs to like, understand, care about and appreciate her emotional needs. In addition, he must be able to relate to her need for passion and sensitivity, to her benevolent side, along with her feminine "nature," and "spirit." He needs to know and like who she *is*, and what she represents in just being a woman. When he sincerely likes all of those things about her, his true love for her will be clearly evident in mind, body and spirit. In other words, to *truely* love a woman, you must first *like and love* her. This same principle also applies to woman as it relates to a man.

As with most things in life, including sex, love and relationships, your reward (of pleasure and happiness) is directly related to how much you're willing to risk (emotionally). So all of you playboys and playgirls out there, I know this may sound a little frightening to most of you, but if you really want to know what a true orgasm really feels like, try having one with a person that you like, trust and are *in* love with.

To find someone you like and also love is a daunting challenge; and though to match the two may be difficult, when you do it's a match made in heaven. And lastly, don't be afraid to love until it hurt—you'll never have pain that feels so good.

Roberto Casanova

Thoughts Of You

This morning at dawn,
I planted some wonderful seeds of thoughts…
Just of You.
I then gazed at your photograph and paused—
Treating my senses to the joy and pleasure that one receives
When seeing your sensuous eyes and beautiful smile.
And from the tears that my new joy brings,
with loving tenderness,
I watered and fertilized my thoughts…
And by the time the moon began to work the nightshift,
My Thoughts Of You
Had blossomed into a magnificent flower…
And like the bumblebee,
I am poised in mid-flight
Ready to drink of your sweet nectar.

R. Ray Barnes

Afterword

"Free falling in love..."

Let Me Say... I Love You

Should the sun ever become too bright,
or the moon fades from sight,
let me not pass up this chance to say,
I Love You.
Should I grow old and my memory fails me, turning cold...
and somehow I forget the splendor of your touch,
let me rush today in saying
I Love You.
Should my life become so hectic, forbid you ever feel rejected,
while I travel more roads than I've expected,
let me say, always,
I Love You.
Should my end of the world one day

F
A
L
L

away
from the place
that happens to be your choice of **s p a c e**,
I wouldn't want to have missed my chance to say
I Love You.

Toi

Afterthought

After having completed **69 Ways To Better Relationships, Sex and Love**, I feel I've learned so much more about love and relationships! I'm astonished by it, though my father would often say, "The more you learn, the more you know... The more you know, the more you learn how much you don't know." Needless to say, I didn't know as much about love and relationships as I thought, and probably still don't. But, I *have* learned that love works better when *you* work with it. Moreover, this experience has given me a vantage point in which to view, understand and appreciate love; it has helped me to realize that the beauty and love within us opens our spirit and awakens our inner-vision to recognize the beauty and love that surrounds us.

Maybe one day we'll all be able to put our various racial, cultural and religious differences aside and use *LOVE* as the common 'inner-denominator' to bring us all together in peace and harmony... Okay, I know that sounds ambitious, but, that's my dream—and I do *know* that dreams can and do come true!

Although writing **69 Ways To Better Relationships, Sex and Love**, hasn't been easy, it *was* very enlightening, fun and every bit a labor of love. In this Afterthought, I want to leave you with a few of my most cherished observations of what my life has revealed to me about love:

- The current worldview seems to suggest that to dislike, despise and hate is rationalized, while to admire, adore and love is marginalized.
- We seem to be having sex a lot more and making love a lot less.
- Innocent flirting while in a relationship is okay.... It feels good to know that you've still got it! Just because you're on a diet doesn't mean you can't look at the menu.
- Love is an "Infinite Voyage," not simply a walk in the park.
- I've noticed that most of us pour our hearts into designing a box that's tailored to fit our pre-conceived notions of our ideal mate; then we frantically search around trying to find that special someone that fits the unique size and shape of the box that we've designed, rather than using our hearts to find that special someone and then designing a box that's tailored to fit *that someone's* unique size and shape.
- Because we don't invest enough time to find out what we truly want in a lover, often times after a few kids, a dog and a mortgage, we discover that we've settled for much less than we imagined our love relationship to be. So, don't rush love.
- I co-opted the profound statement made by the highly regarded spiritual teachers, Dr. Wayne Dyer and Eckhart Tolle: "If you change and seek the greater love that's beyond your 'love situation,' the situation of your love will change."

There Is More To Love Than What Meets The Eye

We've been taught so much as a society to focus on the external beauty of people that we often miss their true beauty, which lies within—as with most of the answers to our love situations. We must stop searching on the outside for a love that lives on the inside.

While physical attractiveness is important and may be a good place to start, without a strong emotional desire to be with that person, admiration, wonderment, like, love and a host of other feelings, it's tantamount to the story of the three pigs, two of whom built their houses out of straw and sticks whereupon any strong wind could blow them down. You can admire the outer beauty, but learn to see and appreciate one's inner beauty; that's a house built of bricks. Building your relationship on looks alone is like having a relationship built of straw and sticks, where any gust of hot air, gossip, rumors or innuendo may cause it to come crashing down. It may be nice to have straw and sticks as exterior decoration, but build your love mansion and its foundation out of bricks and stone.

I've learned that in relationships some things are beyond our control, while others are a matter of choice. Females are female by birth, women by nature and ladies by choice. Similarly, males are male by birth, men by nature and gentlemen by choice.

During the course of my research, I've discovered one thing to be very consistent; most females still prefer to be with gentlemen and most males still prefer to be with ladies. This, at least, gives me some hope that the terms and behaviors associated with "ladies and gentlemen" will not be replaced by "bitches and playas" or "red neck women and honky-tonk men" as some of today's music mantras would suggest.

Keep in mind that it's important, if possible, to enter any new relationship as a *whole* individual, not as one seeking to find your better half. It's best that you both come together whole, then *work* together as *one* to become each other's best half. And, when seeking a mate, *you* should *first* be the person you desire in a mate. So when seeking a partner, before being too critical, as a way of making sure that *you* are the person you desire your *mate* to be, ask yourself, "Would *I* marry *me*?" Also, as many wise teachers have advised, do an autopsy on the death of your last relationship, analyze it and learn from it before giving birth to a new one; this may help you avoid making the same mistakes (in love) over and over again. So, if or when you lose at love, be sure not to lose the lesson of love.

And you must realize that if you're mentally, spiritually and physically healthy, it will have an equal effect on the wellbeing of your love life, sex life and your relationship as a whole. So, choose carefully the battles you wage with your mate. Before you argue and disrupt your calm mental and spiritual state, first decide whether it's more important for you to be "right" or for you to be "at peace and happy." If you choose to be right, make sure your decision is worth the effort and price that it might cost to your state of mind. A few ounces of forethought may save you pounds of grief, mental anguish, wasted energy and an overnight or extended stay on the couch—ultimately getting you "no just-us, no piece…"

Also, when you're in a committed relationship or marriage that needs work, make sure you're not spending more trying to fix up your house than you're spending trying to repair your broken home. You must learn more than how to make a good living together, you must learn how to make a good life together.

Definition Of Love

*If I could **See** the **Look** of **Love**,*
*I **sense** it would be*
*Beautiful, alluring and radiant—like your **Smile**…*
*If I could **Feel** the **Touch** of **Love**,*
*I **sense** it would be*
*Soft, smooth and silky—like your **Skin**…*
*If I could **Hear** the **Sound** of **Love**,*
*I **sense** it would be*
*Melodic, harmonious and rhythmic—like your **Spirit**…*
*If I could **Inhale** the **Scent** of **Love**,*
*I **sense** it would be*
*Sweet-smelling, aromatic and fragrant—like your **Body**…*
*If I could **Taste** the **Flavor** of **Love**,*
*I **sense** it would be*
*Delicious, luscious and everlasting—like your **Kiss**…*
*Having never understood the true **Meaning** of **Love**,*
***Seeing** you, **Touching** you, **Hearing** you, **Smelling** you,*
*and **Tasting** you is the only **Definition Of Love** I need…*

R. Ray Barnes

Remember, in your tireless search for love, no matter what you do or how hard you try, you'll never find "the way to love," because *love is the way*.... And contrary to popular belief, love is not that hard to find—it's really rather easy—you won't need a roadmap, flight plan, OnStar or GPS Navigation; it's much closer than you think. As different as you may perceive each of us to be, if you just chisel away the façade of race, looks, culture, religious attitudes, illusions and beliefs, underneath you'll find that we're all quite the same.... Just pure LOVE.

Seven Principles
To Building A Successful Relationship

Many factors contribute to making a relationship loving and long lasting, but I think there are seven principles or qualities that need be present to ensure the success of the relationship.

- **One: Be Emotionally Free** to **Fall In Love**. Allow yourself the freedom to experience the joy of falling in love without worrying about your pride, ego and *whatever* others may think.
- **Two: Mutual Respect** and **Admiration**. Meaning you are considerate and thoughtful in regards to each other's feelings, and that you have a sense of wonderment toward one another.
- **Three: Trust** and **Honesty**. Meaning each partner is satisfied that the other is "trustworthy," and feels that they can express themselves openly and honestly without fear of reprisal.
- **Four: Good Effective Communication** with **Clear Understanding**. Meaning you talk as well as listen to one another. And after you've conversed, you both come away with a clear understanding of each other's needs, wants and desires.
- **Five: Commitment** and **Dedication**. Meaning each partner must be committed to work through the hard times that are bound to happen when people are engaged in personal relationships, with each partner being truly dedicated to the personal growth and happiness of the other.
- **Six: Be Open Minded** and **Willing** to **Change**. Meaning each partner remains open to new ideas and growth in the

relationship, understanding that the only thing that's constant is change—with each partner willing to make positive changes when necessary.

- **Seven: Practice Forgiveness**. The heaviest thing you can carry is a grudge. Don't worry about who's right and who's wrong; focus on, what's right and what's wrong. So, as soon as possible, cease to feel resentment or anger against your lover for some perceived offense, difference or mistake. Feelings of anger, hatred and animosity toward your lover may leave long lasting negative effects on you and are very injurious to a loving relationship.

If you find that your love relationship lacks these seven qualities, I would advise (if you hope and expect the love to last) that you immediately work on making them a part of your love life, or just move on to a relationship where you *are* able to establish these qualities as the foundation.

And finally, I had an epiphany; I think I have found the key to understanding men and women as it relates to love and commitment. Here's my short "lighthearted" take on both subjects. Let me know what you think.

Email me at: Comments@69WaysTheBook.com.

"Honey, we'll get through this together…"

Understanding Women

Men, women are all about love. It's the essence of their being, and that's all you need to know. Don't try to analyze them, figure them out or even ask why they do the things they do in the manner in which they do them—just accept them. If God can't figure them out at times, neither can you. (Just smile ladies, you know that's true…)

However, know that no matter what the issue or circumstance, you must realize, understand and comprehend that women are *extremely* loving, emotional, sensitive, caring, loyal, supportive, devout and are by far God's greatest blessing—that's why new life is brought forth and nurtured by them and not you. Women are uniquely gifted and truly special! The sooner you come to recognize and accept that fact and work in harmony with her, the rhythm of your love song will move & groove to a much stronger beat. If you ever hope to have a true loving relationship, never underestimate the mind, heart and soul of a woman.

Don't be discouraged by a woman's uncharacteristic approach to doing things, sometimes it makes them appear more complicated than they intend to be. As multifaceted as they are, more than anything women just want to love and be loved—so it's imperative that men reassure women regarding their feelings towards them, in word and deed. It's necessary for women to know how you feel about them, so they can properly direct and fulfill their God-given need and desire to nurture and love. If your behavior indicates that you love them, and they can trust that your love is true, they will willingly, with pleasure and in abundance, bestow all of their love, emotion, sensitivity, caring, loyalty and support upon you—and will be committed to you forever…

Understanding Men

Women, men are all about protecting their manhood, especially physical strength, power, courage, control, attack, defense, greed, fear and resistance which are all a part of their ego. In most aspects of their lives, men *believe* these attributes serve them well; however, some of these characteristics seem in conflict with how men perceive love and commitment. Some men, feeling that love and commitment are a threat to their manhood unwittingly shield their hearts to defend against it and generally seek the least amount of commitment with the maximum amount of benefit. Although their actions may sometimes seem irrational to you," never underestimate the rigidity and stupidity of the male ego. Don't waste your time trying to psychoanalyze them or seek logical answers for their often-illogical behavior. As intelligent and driven as men can be when relating to love, most don't know why they behave the way they do.

With most relationship journeys that could jet men toward a destination of love, they're usually on autopilot with no flight plan. They tend to allow their hearts to wander in and around love aimlessly. In many cases, if men ever find that their hearts have landed in a sea of love and commitment, it shocks their system (which automatically defaults to protecting their manhood) causing them to back away,

"Guys, give 'em credit, women do win------------------sometimes..."

retreat or, in some cases, flee. It's not that they don't want to visit love and commitment; it just frightens them to think of permanently residing there. When this happens to a man that you love (and odds are it will), rather than getting frustrated, women must be patient and show the man the benefits of living in such a wonderful place.

Women must appreciate that God didn't get it quite right with men and created woman as a way to balance what's lacking in man. Yet, when it comes to love, for the balance to be effective, men and women must work together. Translated, this means it will probably be up to women to lead the way. Men are not the best choice when it comes to the emotional aspects of love—they are much better followers. Women are certainly more qualified for that task. Prompting some women to declare, "Men are like mascara, they usually run at the first sign of emotion."

It may seem women shoulder an unfair burden when dealing with men concerning love, but women are endowed with a greater understanding of love and therefore, more responsibility. As Dr. Drew Pinsky said earlier, "…women are more evolved than us guys." Many women seem to agree, comparing men to lava lamps, saying, "They're fun to look at, but not very bright." Think about it. Men have fought major wars over sex. Now how smart is that? So, do you really think God would have men be responsible for fostering and spreading love in the world? One could easily conclude that 'men' are responsible for the many conflicts, the extraordinary amount of violence and *lack* of love that's so evident in the world today.

So, no matter what the issue or circumstance, women must realize that men are well known for concealing their love, pretending to be non-emotional, insensitive, and uncaring. As for men, they think expressing themselves emotionally makes them appear weak and vulnerable. You must remember, men *need* to appear strong, powerful and fearless to protect their manhood. Consequently, women need to pay closer attention to what they say and do when no other men are around to make judgments or cast dispersions on their manhood—then they will generally be more honest, forthright and sincere.

Women should be more influenced by what a man does rather than by what he says. Men often confuse sex *with* love, as well as sex *and* love; however, you mustn't let them confuse you. Some men have no problems lying or seriously misleading women to get what they want. They may deny being married when they are. May say "I love you" when they don't. And may promise to marry you when they won't, just to get you to have sex with them—only for you to find that after you've given in, they've contracted a serious case of amnesia and can't seem to remember anything they've promised or said. So as women, you must consider his *overall* treatment *of* you to gauge his true love *for* you. Unless his words or so-called faith or belief in you is supported by his actions, take it with a grain of salt. Remember, the Bible says in James, Chapter 2: Verse 20, "that faith without works is dead."

The lack of fidelity of married men today is quite astounding and has always been a source of incomprehension for the women who suffer as a result of it. Many women have asked, "Why does my husband cheat?" Throughout history, many married men who possess power, wealth, good looks and/or charisma have had extramarital affairs. Even dating back to the earliest written accounts of sex that were transcribed

"Put your hearts and heads together…"

on the clay tablets of the ancient Sumerians around 3200 BC, there was evidence of men having sex with women other than their wives. And according to professor, Jerrold Cooper of Johns Hopkins University, who stated on a 1999 History Channel Special, *The History of Sex*, "It's clear that there was a patriarchal class society in which women were subservient to men and there were no expectation that the husband would be completely faithful to his wife. That is, men had access to household slaves for sexual purposes and they could frequent prostitutes without any inapproriateness being attached to that." From there the list continues with examples including Ancient Egypt's most infamous Pharaoh, Ramesses The Great, the Biblical Kings, David and Solomon, to recent figures such as former U.S. Presidents, John Kennedy and Bill Clinton, former U.S. Speaker of the House Newt Gingrich, and former and current U.S. Senators Gary Hart, David Vitter, John Edwards, John Ensign and John McCain. Add to this list the former Governors David Paterson and Eliot Spitzer of New York and former Governor Mark Sanford of South Carolina, plus the former New York, Los Angeles and Detroit City Mayors Rudy Giuliani, Antonio Villaraigosa, and Kwame Kilpatrick. And don't forget the Saudi Arabian Oil Sheiks with their harems, Televangelists Jimmy Swaggart and Jim Bakker, actor and comedian Bill Cosby, activist and Minister Jesse Jackson, National Basketball Association superstar Kobe Bryant, professional golf's best ever Eldrick "Tiger" Woods and numerous other famous and not so famous married men have been caught frequenting houses of ill repute and having affairs.

Some of these men do it because of their desire to have "new sex" as we discussed in Part Three, #22 earlier; yet others don't feel comfortable saying and doing the same things with their wives as they do with their girlfriends, harlots, concubines, hookers, streetwalkers, female escorts, chicks on the side, booty calls, call girls, prostitutes or just plain ol' whores. Most of these "vow breakers" are middle to upper class businessmen who can, of course, afford the services of these high priced ladies of the night, ladies of opportunity or collectively some form of the "other woman" and from all indications no matter how much society ridicules her, she's not going anywhere.

An Ebony Magazine August, 2005 exposé had this to say about the notorious *other woman:* "It seems that she has been around since the beginning of time. She is documented in the Bible and on through the days of Julius Caesar, early European royalty, the era of George Washington and Ben Franklin, on through decades to today. She is sometimes referred to as scavenger, seductress, home-wrecker and mindless dreamer, a woman scorned by many a wife and often shunned by those considered to be 'decent churchgoing' people. The other woman can be found in all races and ethnicities, in all income levels and social classes."

This so-called other woman has caused many sexually frustrated and deprived housewives to become 'desperate housewives,' because many of their husbands want to *pretend* to be well behaved church-going men, and as a result seem to have difficulty expressing themselves sexually with what they think to be their 'erotically naive' wives.

Clearly these men mostly see their wives as the mothers of their children, someone with whom they grocery shop, attend church, Bible study, recite prayers and to whom they simply *profess* their love. Lord knows they certainly can't act out their sexual fantasies with such pious women in the same uninhibited way as they do with their highly promiscuous consorts, ladies of the evening or freaky girlfriends.

Some men seem to have trouble talking dirty, being sexually demanding and explicit with what they suppose to be their sweet little innocent wives, yet act quite licentious when it comes to dealing with the *other* woman. In addition, some men claim to feel pressure to "perform" when making love with their wives, yet feel no pressure when having sex with a prostitute or girlfriend. Maybe it's because these women know how to feed their egos, telling them exactly what they want to hear to make them 'feel' like they've just completed a command performance, regardless of how poorly they actually performed. So by the time they leave that other place, the Madame's den, the motel, hotel or wherever they engage in their dastardly deeds, their heads are so huge, before the guilt arrives, that they can hardly get out of the door. Then, they arrive home late to their wives, tired and worn out and claiming they've had such a hard day at work that they just want to go to bed.

I know it's puzzling to see how, when it's convenient, these men can become so 'holier than thou' that they can't allow themselves to talk dirty and act out their sexual desires with their wives, yet are not so holy to find it immoral and reprehensible to have sex, commit adultery and fornicate with these other women—and then, of course, lie about it.

To be perfectly clear, these men are *wrong* for their illicit behavior! And the ladies who knowingly date and perform sexual favors for married men are equally culpable! There is no excuse for either of them! However, despite such culpability, it's being done every day! So the question is, "What's a nice little desperate housewife to do?" First, know that it's not your fault. Men often misbehave badly, all by themselves; but you *can* do something about it. You can hire an investigator and catch him red-handed. You can hire the mob and get him 'bumped and grinded' off. (Just kidding). You could leave him and get divorced, or you could wake up and smell the whipped cream, chocolate syrup, edible panties, scented candles, aromatic baths, fragrant massage oils, etc.

And for some of you very loyal and understanding "vow keepers," it may do you good to take a few pages from the books of these other women and stop acting so sweet and innocent—learn how to be bad sometimes! As Mae West once quipped, "When I'm good I'm very good, but when I'm bad I'm even better!" Remember, all is fair in love and war, especially in the privacy of your own bedroom. Take some hints in male sexual ego boosting from these professional and not so professional women, who are pleasing and sometimes stealing your men.

Ladies, you must promise to let your husbands know that between the sheets, he doesn't have to treat you like "Our Lady Of The Missionary Position." Don't be afraid to demonstrate your willingness and capability to provide him with the same sexual pleasures that he may think he needs to go elsewhere to get. Ultimately, you'll want your husband to experience that same unrestrained, confident, ego-boosting feeling that he gets when having sex with another woman, while at the same time feeling your eagerness, desire, sincere joy, delight and genuine excitement that you have in pleasing him and satisfying the man you love—all of which *can't* be gotten from the other woman.

However, there is no 'one size fits all' for this one. Each husband has to be approached in the way that works best for the both of you. If you want to be happy housewives instead of sexually unfulfilled housewives, take heed.

Even though men may seem hopeless when it comes to fidelity, know that men are fully capable of being committed in love and most truly *want* to be. Believe it or not, the way to a man's heart is actually through his heart—but sometimes you might have to take a detour through his ego and/or his penis. Many men allow their egos to overshadow their hearts and their intellect, making it difficult for them to recognize true love and express love in the same straightforward manner that feels so natural for women. From a man's point of view, it seems in discord with his manhood. When it comes to love and expressing love—I know it's sad but true—men are often confused and need guidance.

Many men are like the dog that chases the car: when he catches it he doesn't know what to do with it; so he begins to walk away—only to go chase the next car that comes along—and he will continue to do this over and over again.... So, you women who are driving the car must sometimes open the door (with your love) so that he knows you want him to come inside—and on most occasions he will jump inside, sit on the backseat, wag his tail, stick his tongue out, pant, lick you all over, protect you from other dogs and go willingly wherever your love takes him—and all you need do is let him stick his head out the window occasionally so he can get some air.... Because, according to the Chinese proverb, "Wife who *keep* husband in doghouse, soon find him in cat house."

I sincerely hope that what I've written will have a positive effect on your love life. I wish my words to be beams that illuminate the dark hidden recesses of your heart and soul—those often-neglected places deep inside us that rarely see the light of day or the glow of *true* love. I truly hope that *69 Ways To Better Relationships, Sex and Love* has helped to brighten and awaken that everlasting love that's deep inside you... and that at the very least these words made you smile. I pray that every loving relationship that you are involved in serves as a bridge that leads you to a greater understanding of love, and subsequently to a pathway that leads you to even more fulfilling love relationships.

However, if all has failed, remember that the end of a relationship precedes a new beginning....

Wherever Your Love Takes Me

I thought I wanted to go to
Disney World, Magic Mountain, and Cedar Point—
Some magical, wild and wonderful places,
Where I could really enjoy myself and have lots of fun...
I thought maybe even a trip to
Hawaii, Jamaica and Aruba—
Some blissful island paradise,
Where I could walk along the beach
And just play in the sand all day...
I thought too about a journey into
The Brazilian Rain Forest—
Where I could truly sojourn with nature,
To observe some of the most marvelous wonders
That the Creator has afforded us...
I thought about an exploration to
The Arctic Circle—
Where I could experience first hand
The breathtaking and amazing
White Nights and Northern Lights...
I gave serious thought about taking
An African Safari—
Camping at the foothills of Kilimanjaro

And maybe even an adventurous trip across
The mighty sands of the Sahara...
I thought about touring the
Great ruins of Greece and Rome—
Riding a Gondola in Venice,
Seeing Paris from the top of the Eiffel Tower
And hanging-out at The Louvre with Vincent Van Gogh...
I also thought about going to
Nepal—
Just to take a helicopter ride
To get a great view from the top of the world at Mount Everest.
Then descending to the ocean's bottom
To that mysterious place where even sunlight has never been,
To behold bioluminescent fish with no eyes,
And Jellyfish that know nothing of peanut butter...
I thought about painting the town in
Hollywood, San Francisco, New York, Tokyo,
Montreal and Las Vegas—
And even taking an up close view of
The Grand Canyon, Niagara Falls, The Taj Mahal and
The Great Pyramids of Egypt...
But, more than wanting to do all those things,
I desire mostly to be wherever you are—
Traveling deep within your heart,
And holding you tightly around my spirit,
On a journey of Love, Joy, Peace, Trust and Understanding,
And going happily
Wherever Your Love Takes Me...

R. Ray Barnes

About The Authors

R. Ray Barnes, Author, Poet, Actor & Lecturer
(aka Roberto Casanova & Julie Lovelace)

Originally from Detroit, Michigan, Ray is an author, poet, lecturer and an accomplished record producer, songwriter and Executive Manager of In Spirit International, LLC, an entertainment and publishing company. He has written for the screen, stage, created a successful biblical board game, *Resurrection: The Life of Christ*, and currently has projects in development for film, stage and television.

Roberto Casanova

Roberto is a former "playboy" who turned "lover." During his exploits as a playboy he discovered that he often took advantage of the kind, loving hearts and trusting nature of women by being dishonest and cunning to cover up his infidelity.

Once exposed, most of the beautiful women that he had made love to and had relationships with, often despised him for misusing and abusing their love and causing the relationships to end in despair.

But unexpectedly, like the proverbial case of the 'hunter getting captured by the game', while still a playboy Roberto made the grave error of falling in love. She loved him, too. However, after having gotten tired of his playboy ways she called it off and Roberto was heartbroken. Being so devastated in the process, he decided to give up being a playboy and became a *real* lover of women instead.

As a lover, Roberto began to show care, respect and concern for women. He no longer took advantage of them and found their response to be quite the contrary from that of his playboy days. After making his transition from playboy to lover, most of the beautiful women that he made love to simply adored him. Even after their relationships were over many still loved him and would often reminisce about how wonderful he treated them and they continue to call on him today for advice in their present relationships–planting the seed for *69 Ways To Better Relationships, Sex and Love*.

Several very wealthy women whom he had loving relationships with offered to take care of him and make him their "boy-toy." Yet to date, Roberto has respectfully declined. Instead, he decided to help write *69 Ways To Better Relationships, Sex and Love* as a way to share his vast knowledge of sex, relationships and love with the many who wish to elevate themselves and become great lovers like him.

Julie Lovelace

Julie was a former "high class lady of the night" who often found herself being more of a sex therapist than a sex goddess. Surprisingly, most of her clients were married businessmen with families. After she would satisfy them sexually, she discovered she was spending more time answering questions from her 'Johns' about how they could get their wives to say and do the things that she does.

After a while, she found she was having more counseling sessions than she was having sex. The advice and suggestions she had given her clients about the things they could say and do to have better sex with their wives worked so well, she eventually lost most of her clientele. The wives of many of her former Johns were now satisfying them at home. This wonderful turn of events forced Julie to question whether she should *stay* in the sex business she loved so well.

With more advice seeking customers than those seeking sex, Julie decided to collaborate with Roberto to write 69 *Ways To Better Relationships, Sex and Love,* so that other men *and* women could benefit from some of the techniques she learned and acquired while working in the field talking to men about their sexual desires and how they preferred to be sexually pleased, treated and satisfied.

You may contact R. Ray Barnes, Roberto Casanova and Julie Lovelace via email at rraybarnes@69WaysTheBook.com.

About The Contributors

With all the gratitude I have, I would like to personally acknowledge our physician consultant, Dr. Karen M. Webster and photographer, LaSalle Barnes whose contributions helped to make 69 *Ways To Better Relationships, Sex and Love* such a very special and unique project.

Dr. Karen M. Webster, M.D., MPH

Dr. Karen Webster is a Women's Health Specialist who received her M.D. and her Master's degree in Public Health from the Johns Hopkins University School of Medicine and the Johns Hopkins University School of Public Health. Her life's work has focused on the care of women and children, particularly those who are under-insured and medically under-served. She is passionately involved in Women's Reproductive Rights and the diagnosis and management of premalignant conditions of the cervix. She is currently the Medical Director of the

B St. Health Center in Sacramento, California. As a former dancer, she is a lover of the arts as well as a fitness enthusiast and marathon runner. Dr. Webster resides in Northern California with her devoted husband and children.

LaSalle Barnes

LaSalle Barnes is one of the most creative and sought after photographers to recently surface on the Los Angeles photographic landscape. LaSalle is regularly called upon to photograph some of Hollywood's most well known TV, film and music stars, as well as high fashion models and celebrity sports figures. He's also an official photographer for Hollywood's World Famous Magic Castle, the private clubhouse for the Academy of Magical Arts, and showplace for some of the greatest magicians from around the globe. In addition, he's a very skilled and talented graphic artist as well. To explore more of LaSalle's photographic works, please visit www.lasallebarnesphotography.com. With regards to photography in the book, please send emails to Comments@69WaysTheBook.com.

About The Poets

I think all of us are truly poets at heart, it's only that some of us choose to write our ideas down, while most just live our poems. I would like to sincerely thank all the poets for allowing us to share in their thoughts, dreams, fantasies and ideas. Their words are the thread that binds the whole book together.

Bianca Baker

Bianca loves to write poetry. She works in the public relations field and is a freelance writer who has written articles for several national publications.

Denise L. Cook, The Oracle

Denise L. Cook, known as "The ORACLE," is an award winning Author, Motivational Speaker, Actor, Poet, Singer/Songwriter, Choreographer and Dancer. Denise holds a B.A. in Dance and M.F.A. from U.C.L.A and M.ED. from National University. She received her teaching credential from the Graduate School of Education at U.C.L.A.

Her literary accomplishments include her newly released book and R&B, Jazz, Spoken Word Fusion music CD, *The Oracle Speaks… just because* and her first book *Full Circle Balance In Life:* A collection of poetry and prose chronicling self-love and self-awareness. She's also been a featured vocalist on several music CD's for musicians and recording artists well known to the Los Angeles music scene and nationally as well.

Ms. Cook is a celebrated philanthropist, noted for her unending volunteerism at Hollywood High Performing Arts Center, and is a Board Member and Director of Publicity and Public Affairs for Performing Arts For Life Education Foundation, a non-profit organization dedicated to bringing the arts to the inner city and under-served youth of Los Angeles, CA.

Leslie E. Pogue

Leslie Pogue is an Independent Consultant who speaks publicly and hosts scheduled workshops on managing Depression and Anxiety. As well as being a poet and writer, she creates and facilitates training modules targeted at corporate and specialized needs.

Saphron

Poet, writer, spoken word artist, and health educator, Saphron creates positive, sensual imagery from a woman's perspective. Her landmark work *"A Chocolate Taste"* achieved international recognition not only for the luscious imagery it embodies, but the dialog and openness it inspires. Saphron helps women own their desire and gain a vocabulary through which to express their deepest longings.

Of special note is the work she does with breast cancer survivors, and other women recovering from trauma. Her popular workshops help women reclaim their sexuality as they heal from their health challenges. This visionary work garnered the prestigious "Buzzy Award" in 2002 for Outstanding Sex Educator.

Her wonderful and timely book, *"Recipes for Good Lovin"* coinsides very nicely with 69 Ways. For more information on Saphron's books and workshops, contact ladysaphron@yahoo.com.

Lisa Stout

Lisa, an avid lover and writer of poetry and prose, is a graduate of Michigan State University. She's the mother of three beautiful daughters and currently works in the Healthcare field.

Toi

Toi is a dynamic motivational speaker, poet, writer, education/employment consultant, Certified Life Coach, professional mom and word-meister at large. Her greatest pastime is inspiring others to not only *think* outside of the box but to shed the box altogether!

Regarding any of the poems or poets featured in the book, you may write via email to Comments@69WaysTheBook.com.

"A park, flowers, champagne, pillows, a blanket and you—priceless!"

Acknowledgments

*A*s authors and publishers of this book, we would like to acknowledge and give our sincere thanks and gratitude to the following people. All contributed in more than 69 ways. Without their individual efforts and support, this book would not have been possible and we appreciate them from the bottom of our hearts. We would like to offer an extra special thanks to Elaine R. Redus and Cecelia E. Finney for their tireless effort and personal commitment to making this book the best it could be, an inspirational thanks to Oprah Winfrey and a personal thanks to Lois E. Moore.

Ron Kenner	Pam Moore	Carol Meade
Barbara Acevedo	Yvette Merritt	Joyce Harris
Jeannetta Stitt	Bette Tate-Beaver	Mercedes Baca
Bessie Haynes	Cheryl Murphy	Momilanii Kauakahi
LaSalle Barnes	Sandy Jackson	Diane Rhodes
Mona M. Holland	Nina Adams	Tina Jackson
Wanda Smith	Michelle McGhee	Prentis Byrd
Jaaz Jones	Julie Smith	Lamont McClemore
Tony Coleman	Elese Barnes	Nedra Sneed
Thecla McCulloh	Julie Delgado	Bethene Lee
Gina Stallworth	Annette Mohammed	Velicia Ervin
Patricia Lang	Bahni Turpin	Sherrema Pearson

Leslie Franklin	Larry Lerma	Karla Wallace
Mimi Wethers-Smith	Sheila Gilmore	Marcus Lowe
Marsel Watts	Florence Souder	Leslie Graves
Tim Lyon	Becky Williams	LaFrancine Tate
Vickie McAlpine	Robin L. Burns	Renee E. Cobb
Sonya Wilson	Donna Taliaferro	Joyce O'Riley
Bonita Patterson	Tarrie Adams	Colette Williams
Sheila Muhammad	Christina Chen	Symone Carter
Nedra Jones	Tim Owens	C. Tillery Banks
Connie Gresham	Bethany Richardson	Damon Ritchie
Toiya Tucker	Claudia Ilcken	Angela DeJoseph
Marlo Aubert	Faye Bernard	Kimberly Pattio

Finding Love

Don't go seeking to
FIND **Love***,*
because if you can
find something you can lose it…
Seek to
BE **Love**
by recognizing and becoming one with
THE **Love**
within you—
then,
you'll never be without **It***…*
and all others who
ARE **Love**
will find
You

R. Ray Barnes

Sources, Suggested Reading, and Related Websites

The following lists of books and authors were great resources and comparative references in the writing of **69 Ways To Better Relationships, Sex and Love**. If you are seeking a more in-depth analysis and understanding of sex, relationships and love along with the spirituality needed to truly love and be *in* love, we highly recommend and endorse their reading.

Sex, Relationships and Love

The Complete Idiot's Guide To Amazing Sex
    By Sari Locker
Sex: A Man's Guide
    By Stefan Bechtel & Laurence Roy Stains
Tantric Secrets *(7 Steps To The Best Sex Of Your Life)*,
    By Cassandra Lorius
A Lifetime of Sex
    By Stephen C. George & Ken Winston Caine
The New Joy of Sex
    Alex Comfort, M. B., D.Sc.
Ultimate Sex
    Judy Bastyra

Sassy, Single, & Satisfied
  Michelle McKinney Hammond
The Dr. Phil Show
  Dr. Phillip C. McGraw
    Website: www.drphil.com
Strictly Sex With Dr. Drew (DHC)
  Dr. Drew Pinsky
    Website: www.discoveryhealth.com

Spirituality and Love

Sexuality and Spirituality
  By Yogi Bhajan, Ph.D. & Gururattan Kaur Khalsa, Ph.D.
    Website: www.yogatech.com or www.yogibhajan.com
The Seven Spiritual Laws of Success
  By Deepak Chopra
    Website: www.chopra.com
The Power Of Now
(A Guide To Spiritual Enlightenment)
  By Eckhart Tolle
    Website: www.eckharttolle.com
The Power Of Intention
  By Dr. Wayne Dyer
    Website: www.drwaynedyer.com
The Prophet* and *Secrets of the Heart
  By Kahlil Gibran
    Website: www.kahlil.org
The Four Agreements
(A Practical Guide to Personal Freedom)
  By Don Miguel Ruiz
    Website: www.miquelruiz.com

Health Related Websites

In developing the "**Healthful Hints**," for **69 Ways To Better Relationships, Sex and Love**, the following websites were extremely helpful and informative. Please visit them for a more comprehensive look into maintaining good sexual health and better health overall.

Dr. Dean Edell
   Website: www.healthcentral.com
CDC National Prevention Information Network
   Website: www.cdcnpin.org
American Social Health Association
   Website: www.ashastd.org
Mayo Clinic
   Website: www.MayoClinic.com
Diseases of the prostate and their treatments
   Website: www.Prostate.com
American Urological Association
   Website: www.UrologyHealth.org
American Cancer Society
   Website: www.cancer.org
American Obesity Association
   Website: www.obesity.org
United States government's new food pyramid
   Website: www.MyPyramid.gov
American Heart Association
   Website: www.americanheart.org
American Lung Association
   Website: www.Lungusa.org
United States Department of Health & Human Services
   Website: www.hhs.gov
Ask Men Online Magazine
   Website: www.AskMen.com
The Sexual Health Information Center
   Website: www.sexhealth.org
American Academy of Physicians
   Website: www.familydoctor.org
E Medicine Consumer Health
   Website: www.emedicinehealth.com

Dating Match Makers
Website: www.DatingMatchMakers.com
Body Fitness Top Resources of the Net
Website: www.bodyfitness.com

Internet Dating Websites

For those of you who may want to venture into the realm of online dating, we recommend the following websites. If you have a unique or personal dating service need or requirement, use search engines such as Google.com, Yahoo.com or Bing.com to locate the specific types of dating websites you may be seeking.

Chemistry
Website: www.chemistery.com
Match
Website: www.match.com
Zoosk.com
Website: www.Zoosk.com
Spark.com
Website: www.Spark.com
Perfect Match
Website: www.PertectMatch.com
eHarmony
Website: www.eharmony.com
Plenty Of Fish
Website: www.pof.com
Black People Meet
Website: www.BlackPeopleMeet.com
Ok Cupid
Website: www.okcupid.com
Christian Mingle
Website: www.christianmingle.com
Our Time
Website: www.ourtime.com

Song of Solomon

We've all heard the saying, "All good things come to those who wait." And for enduring to the very end, we reward your steadfastness and patience with this special surprise treat. Many of you may not have realized that sensual and erotic love has been a part of human expression since the beginning of time—as is shown in this beautiful poetic chapter of the *Holy Bible's Old Testament* or *Hebrew Bible*, purportedly written some 3000 years ago.

Song of Solomon, Chapter 7

Young Man:

1. How beautiful are your feet in sandals, O prince's daughter! The curves of your thighs are like jewels, the work of a skilled craftsman.
2. Your navel is as delicious as a goblet filled with wine. Your waist is lovely, like a bundle of wheat encircled by lilies.
3. Your breasts are like twin fawns of a gazelle.
4. Your neck is as stately as an ivory tower. Your eyes sparkle like the pools of Heshbon by the gate of Bath-Rabbim. Your nose is beautiful like Mount Lebanon above the city of Damascus.

5. Thine head upon thee is like Carmel,
   Your hair is like royal tapestry; the king is held captive by its tresses.
6. How beautiful and how pleasant you are, O love, with your delights!
7. You stand like a palm tree. And your breasts are like its fruit.
8. I said, 'I will go to the top of the palm tree. I will take hold of its branches.' O, may your breasts be like the fruit of the vine, and the sweet smell of your breath like apples.
9. And the roof of thy mouth like the best wine for my beloved,

Young Woman:

Wine that goeth down sweetly,
causing the lips of those that are asleep to speak.
10. I am my beloved's, and his desire is toward me.
11. Come, my beloved, let us go forth into the field;
    let us lodge in the villages.
12. Let us get up early to the vineyards;
    let us see if the vine flourish, whether the tender grape appear, and the pomegranates bud forth: there will I give thee my loves.
13. The mandrakes give a smell, and at our gates are all manner of pleasant fruits, new and old,
    which I have laid up for thee, O my beloved.

For those of you who may have thought that exploring each other sensually was in some way unholy, this 7th Chapter of *The Song Of Solomon* is testament that it is not. To *love* and *be loved* is always sacred....

This special version of Chapter 7 of The Song of Solomon was composed of the following translations of the Old Testament of The Holy Bible: Kings James Version, (KJV) Public Domain, New King James Version, (NKJV) © 1982 by Thomas Nelson, Inc., New International Version, (NIV) © 1973, 1978, 1984 by International Bible Society, New Living Translation, (NLT) © 1996 by Tyndale Charitable Trust, Contemporary English Version, (CEV) © 1995 by American Bible Society and the New Life Version, (NLV) © 1969 by Christian Literature International.

"Ooh this love is nice!"

Recognizing True Love

True Love is a full course meal that includes an appetizer, main course and dessert; and no matter how it's served—fresh, raw, boiled, baked, barbequed, fried, sautéed, steamed, stewed, slow cooked, smothered, charbroiled, grilled or blackened—it will be seasoned to your liking, nourishing and fulfilling. If not, it's not true love...

True Love will always make you stronger and lift you higher.... So, if you find yourself feeling weak and tired with a love that's hovering low to the ground, examine it closely and you'll discover it's not true love....

True Love is not something that you "fall into," but a love that you ascend to.

R. Ray Barnes

Final Thought

How Do You Know You're In Love?

*If, when you **hold** her hand it **touches** her heart—*
*If, when you **caress** her body you **embrace** her soul—*
*If, when you **embrace** her soul it **touches** <u>your</u> heart,*
__trembles__ <u>your</u> body
*and **stirs** <u>your</u> Soul…*
　　　　　—Then you know you're In Love.

R. Ray Barnes

Lets toast: "The best things in life are free—you and me together…"

Contact Us

E-MAIL Us at: Love@69WaysTheBook.com
E-MAIL COMMENTS to: Comments@69WaysTheBook.com

ONLINE ORDERS please go to
https://www.createspace.com/4416945 or
www.69WaysTheBook.com
and click the ORDER button

For INFORMATION, BOOKINGS and READINGS
Please E-MAIL Us at: Love@69WaysTheBook.com
Or call toll free 855.6.69.WAYS or 855.669.9297

Please mail any correspondence to:
IN SPIRIT INTERNATIONAL, LLC.
69 Ways The Book
P.O. Box 571633, Los Angeles, CA 91357

www.69WaysTheBook.com

Facebook.com/69WaysTheBook

Twitter.com/69WaysTheBook

www.ingramcontent.com/pod-product-compliance
Lightning Source LLC
Chambersburg PA
CBHW071704090426
42738CB00009B/1651